OUR MEANINGLESS EXISTENCE

Ideas from Philosophy That
Change the Way You Think

ROBERT PANTANO

of Pursuit of Wonder

CONTENTS

PREFACE

My interest in philosophy started where I'd imagine it starts for most people: a dissatisfaction with what I had been told about life combined with a curiosity about what I had not.

I remember the feeling when I first read a collection of essays by Ralph Waldo Emerson. I remember thinking *yes, this is it. This is what I've been looking for.* Then the same happened with Dostoyevsky, with Camus, with Schopenhauer, with Pessoa, with Wallace, and so on. Throughout my life, philosophy and literature have given me a way to confront my concerns, thoughts, questions, and doubts, without the tiptoeing and masquerading I often experienced in other areas of life and *self-development*. Continually, I found the earnestness of writers and thinkers providing me with a feeling of mutual respect and understanding because, for the first time, I felt I was being offered attempts at truth that were closer to my experience of life. They were bold, direct, and unwavering.

Throughout the years, I've realized how common it is to feel like something is missing and that there must be more behind everything. So many of us feel as though we have been given a carcass of life, of meaning, that is covered by a blanket of falsity and ignorance. There is a need for a type of food that nourishes the mind and *spirit*—a food that people from all around the world and at all times in history have contributed small but notable servings of in the form of *philosophy* and *art*. As I've studied and learned more about these subjects, I've felt an increasing obligation to help provide for others what was provided to me: access to these crucial servings of intellectual sustenance. I've felt the need to translate, share, and contribute to the conversations I have had with books, films, videos, and art, as I understand them. This book is a collection of essays that have been written as part of this effort.

The essays originally appeared in video form on my YouTube channel, Pursuit of Wonder—but the YouTube channel was originally formed out of a book that got rejected by publishers and agents. Since I couldn't find a traditional distribution channel, I took the manuscript of the book and turned each section into videos. Those videos were the beginning of the Pursuit of Wonder YouTube channel, a project that has developed and evolved into something that is beyond my ability to comprehend. In full circle, I have now begun and hope to continue sharing my work in print as well as other media.

Pursuit of Wonder started as a longing to relentlessly pursue my curiosity toward wonder and truth. It then turned into a sense of obligation to write and create the most interesting and useful content I could, based on what I found. And now, it has turned into a source of great meaning for me. Through the process, I have formed a new relationship with the world in one of its greatest lights—a community of those interested in truth, in living well, and in pursuing wonder. I hope you find something in this work, and in my work more broadly, that might assist in your own process of discovering meaning just the same.

PART I

THE ESSENCE
OF WONDER

The first selection of essays begins where philosophy both began in time and begins for the individual—at the intersection of wonder and meaninglessness; the point at which our curiosity meets its match in a futile, indifferent, chaotic, and absurd universe.

At the moment of self-consciousness and inquiry into the world, we are fated to ask questions like: *how does the world work? Why does it work this way? What does it mean to be me? How do I deal with these questions and their seemingly unanswerable nature?* It is these questions that we find at the bottom of philosophy and at the top of the descent into meaninglessness—a descent that we must arguably make, because if we have already explored any of these questions or intuitions, we have already begun down this path, and it is too late to turn around and unknow what we now know. And so, the key is not to stop but to continue down and onward in order to find a new ground of existence in which we can bear and live comfortably with *truth*, or the lack thereof.

The following essays touch on this process and how various ancient philosophies from both the East and West can be used and applied today toward living a worthwhile and meaningful life, despite life's uncertain conditions.

THE WONDER OF THE UNKNOWN

In our everyday life, most things are generally considered normal and routine—a tree, a bird, a drive home from work, a meal, a load of laundry, a night's sleep, and so on. At a certain age of adolescence, most things begin to fall into the category of being rather unexciting or tedious. This can, for obvious reasons, pose problems for our experience of life. It can produce a frequent sense of boredom and monotony.

Science, religions, and philosophies often work to provide us with answers and clarity about the universe and our existence within it. We seek to learn about what we, as a collective species, know about ourselves and this reality in order to improve our experience of it. This can be helpful, of course, but perhaps an equally valuable and often neglected source of wisdom, joy, and vitality can be found not in what we know but in what we don't know. Nineteenth-century writer Henry David Thoreau wrote:

My desire for knowledge is intermittent; but my desire to commune with the spirit of the universe, to be intoxicated with the fumes, call it, of that divine nectar, to bear my head through atmospheres and over heights unknown to my feet, is perennial and constant.

In other words, the experience and effects of concrete knowledge can be fleeting, but the wonder found in the spirit of the unknown can be constant and enduring. With no more than a glance upward at a clear, starry night sky, as we stare into the eyes of the incomprehensible and infinite space above us, we are likely to experience an overwhelming awareness of how little we know and how little we are. The universe stares back at us with its stark glare and reminds us how deeply strange and unclear our life really is, even the most simple and normal things. The great cosmologist Carl Sagan said, "The Cosmos is all that is or was or ever will be. Our feeblest contemplations of the Cosmos stir us—there is a tingling in the spine, a catch in the voice, a faint sensation, as if a distant memory, of falling from a height." This feeling of awe is immensely liberating and provoking. It reminds us that we stand at the crossroads of the infinite and the finite, everything and nothing, knowledge and unawareness.

In truth, no matter what we think we know, we are probably wrong, and no matter what anyone else thinks they know, they are probably wrong. No one knows what's going on in any fundamental sense. Nothing about this life is simple or clear, and from the perspective of the stars, nothing down here on earth—including us—matters all that much to anything beyond itself. Paradoxically, in this, we find great opportunity for wisdom, humility, exploration, and profound experience in our lives. "Nobody ever figures out what life is all about, and it doesn't matter. Explore the world. Nearly everything is really interesting if you go into it deeply enough," said renowned theoretical physicist Richard Feynman.

In even the most common and mundane things, there is complexity and strangeness. We don't even know why we sleep or dream. We don't know how most of our brain works or what consciousness is. We don't know if time is real in any physical sense. We don't know what gravity is or why it is. We don't know if there are infinite other universes or dimensions around us. We don't know why energy or matter even came to be in the first place—or why it was followed by a perfect sequence of colliding, combining, exploding, and emerging, all to put us here, right now, able to ask why.

At the base of almost everything, the resulting truth is this: *we don't know*. When we disregard this unknowingness, we can easily become disinterested, uninspired, and worn out of this life. We can put great stress on things that perhaps don't matter all that much and neglect experiences and things that do. We can feel the pressure and anxiety of chasing perfection and certainty, which do not exist.

We should look to the universe often, not solely for answers but for perspective; for a helpful adjustment and an aerial consideration of our daily life. With this practice, the little things in life become more striking, the mistakes and the annoyances become less significant, the calm comes more easily, and the everyday activities of our lives that we so often view as wasteful and tedious reveal themselves to be wonderfully strange and curious parts of our existence that we should make effort to ponder and appreciate as often as we can. As if to say, *I'd love to marvel at and enjoy this work of art I've created,* the universe gave itself humanity. "Through our eyes, the universe is perceiving itself. Through our ears, the universe is listening to its harmonies. We are the witnesses through which the universe becomes conscious of its glory, of its magnificence," said twentieth-century American-British philosopher Alan Watts. What a shame it would be to waste this experience by failing to appreciate the glory and magnificence found in the unknown.

We must try to remember as often as we can that the unknown permeates everything. Its wonder is always above us, below us, around us, and inside us, whenever we need it.

WHY INTELLIGENT PEOPLE BECOME PESSIMISTIC

Starting from the instant we form an awareness of the world, all the way up until the final second before we die, we will without doubt experience many moments in which life goes very wrong; moments where a friend betrays us, where we make a big mistake or fail at something we worked really hard at, where someone we love decides they no longer feel the same for us or we no longer feel the same for them, moments where we lose someone close far too early, and so on. From small to big, annoying to tragic, there will continue to be moments where our *self*, the world, and humanity appear to all be in complete conflict and disarray.

At a very young age, life seems to be mostly candy, playgrounds, cartoon mice, and fun. The universe feels like it is made for us. Throughout childhood, things in popular culture like movies, TV shows, and advertising reinforce this hopeful optimism by selling us ideals of a life filled with easy friendships, love at first sight, exciting lifestyles, successful and fulfilling careers, and cool products that will all culminate in a perfect, smooth life. Of course, as we grow further past our youthful innocence, the world increasingly reveals itself to be far more complicated and convoluted. As we experience more of life, and we are continually disappointed by our optimism's inability to align with the real conditions of the world, our optimism is beaten further and further into submission.

At this point, the individual is often compelled to surrender any form of naïve optimism and replace it with some degree of pessimism. Arguably, any honestly examined life goes through this transition. At first, this might sound rather somber and bleak, and if we stop here, it very well can be. However, with the proper consideration, perhaps there is a way in which we can leverage this pessimism and use it to our advantage. Perhaps there is a way through pessimism that leads to an adapted and more reasonable optimism—not the sort of delusional optimism that is ignorant to the somber truths of our condition, but rather, an optimism that exists in spite of it all.

Arguably, all great philosophies and religions incorporate some degree of pessimism in their foundations. What reason would philosophies and religions have to exist if they did not first admit the existence of the pains, confusions, and uncertainties of life? The philosophy of Stoicism suggests that the universe is indifferent to what we want from it. Buddhism says that *life is suffering*. Existentialism and Absurdism say that we are stricken by our need for meaning in a life that is inherently meaningless. Christianity proclaims that the condition of humankind is inflicted with temptation and imperfection. Along with many others, these schools of thought realize that life contains fundamental pessimisms. However, what is powerful, important, and lasting about any good philosophy or frame of thinking is what it attempts to do with these pessimisms. A helpful philosophy first realizes and admits the sad, troublesome, and often tragic conditions of our life, and then attempts to grapple with and overcome them so that we might live in spite of those conditions.

A healthy dose of pessimism is necessary in our ability to adequately deal with this life. It helps us mitigate our expectations and serves as padding that protects us from life's constant attempts to beat our spirit out of us. Pessimism counterbalances the ridiculously overly optimistic expectations of the culture we live in and helps us adapt out of the deeply detached, unrealistic perspective that we likely formed as children. It reminds us that things won't always go our way or always be that nice, but rather, things will go wrong a lot, but despite this, we can still be ok. Paradoxically, we must recognize that through a certain quality of pessimism, we can better arrive at a more reasonably optimistic experience of life.

We are all struggling and improvising our way through this strange existence, constantly confused and unsure. No one is perfect or normal in any traditional sense. No one knows who or why they are. We all make mistakes, big and small. Happiness is hard and unclear. There appears to be no achievement, material item, or endgame that can solve all the problems we face as individuals or as a species. There is greed, tragedy, and malevolence in this world that we have and will continue to experience. And at any moment, our lives could end—this whole world and humanity could end—and at some moment, they will certainly end. But despite everything that was just said, the thought of it all ending should and does make us sad and tremble with fear. We don't want it to end. Despite the chaos, uncertainties, and hardships, we want to go on, we want to endure, we want to see what we can do, overcome, and experience in the face of it all. In this, we find the hopeful spirit and strength of humankind. We find the optimism in the pessimism.

This game of reality appears to have rules; some that we can understand and tamper with, most of which we cannot; some that work in our favor, plenty that do not. Where these rules come from and why they are the way they are is completely and utterly unclear. What is clear, however, is that at this moment, they are, and because they are, we are. To be completely optimistic about the rules always working in our favor would be foolish. However, to be completely pessimistic about the game as a whole simply because the rules don't always work in our favor would be equally foolish. Would a game where the rules always work in the players favor even be a game at all? Of what interest would this be? What experience would there be to have? To give up on life entirely would be like refusing to play a game because we lose sometimes, as if the game would even be worth playing if we knew we were going to win every time we played. There is courage in facing the realities of pessimism and there is strength to be formed in its name. We must be pessimistic about life's conditions in order to face their realities, but we must also be optimistic about our ability to face their realities and form strength, meaning, and experience through them.

Pessimism is real. It is natural. It is helpful. But it is not all there is. Like dirt is to flowers, like darkness is to light, and like silence is to song, pessimism is to optimism. Rather than being optimistic about the possibility of finding things and ideas that will rid us and our lives of disorder, defectiveness, confusion, and vulnerability, perhaps we should attempt to be optimistic about the potential value that we can find in accepting and enduring these things. We should be optimistic about our ability to turn the ups-and-downs into an interesting and beautiful ride.

In the dirt of life, it is up to us to plant the seeds, watch the flowers grow, and enjoy their beauty, even in spite of the fact that we know that they will die.

WISDOM BEGINS WITH KNOWING YOU KNOW NOTHING

The Philosophy of Socrates & Plato

Known as the father of Western philosophy, the ancient Greek philosopher Socrates is regarded as one the most influential thinkers in history. Encouraging and shaping the early budding of philosophy and directly inspiring other formative ancient Greek philosophers like Plato and Aristotle, Socrates would be a catalyst for the way humanity has thought and continues to think about the world and the way we live within it.

There are no known written works directly attributed to Socrates, so he remains a fairly mysterious figure. All accounts of his life and philosophy are provided by other classical writers, many of which differ and sometimes contradict each other. In historical studies, this is what is known as the Socratic problem:

the fact that it is difficult, if not impossible, to fully pin down an accurate picture of what he believed. However, most of what is understood and believed to be accurate is found in the work of his most famous student, Plato, who would go on to become an essential figure in Socrates' legacy as well as for the development of Western philosophy in general, writing around thirty-six books, all comprised of dialogues primarily featuring Socrates.

It is generally agreed that Socrates was born in Athens in Ancient Greece in around 469 BC. It is believed that his philosophical occupation began after a successful career as a stonemason and having fought with distinction in the Athenian military during the Peloponnesian war. During this later, philosophically-focused part of his life, Socrates spent most of his time wandering around Athens, asking lots of questions, and challenging lots of men who the public believed to be wise. He would soon become very skeptical of the so-called wisdom of the time, finding that most men who claimed wisdom and were held to be wise were essentially just arrogant. In Plato's book, *Apology*, Socrates has this to say about his interaction with one particular wise man:

> ...conversing with him, this man seemed to me to seem to be wise to many other people and especially to himself, but not to be so; and then I tried to show him that he thought he was wise, but was not. As a result, I became hateful to him and to many of those present; and so, as I

went away, I thought to myself, "I am wiser than this man; for neither of us really knows anything fine and good, but this man thinks he knows something when he does not, whereas I, as I do not know anything, do not think I do either. I seem, then, in just this little thing to be wiser than this man at any rate, that what I do not know I do not think I know either."

It was this that Socrates believed separated him from others of the time and defined true wisdom. Arguably, he was right, as this credo would ultimately become one of the defining components of a legacy that has lasted for millennia while the philosophies of other wise men of the time have faded into obscurity.

Socrates would go on to spend much of his time attempting to teach and convince others to question what they held to be true, and realize, as he put it, that "[t]he only true wisdom is knowing you know nothing." In doing so, he believed he would compel others to join him on a journey of philosophical inquiry toward a better life as they realized their current answers and beliefs were insufficient.

As time passed, Socrates would garner a following of young students interested in his way of thinking. Although he was skeptical of knowledge and popular ideas, he was not without convictions. He taught and made claims about politics, being extremely critical of democracy; he made assessments of values, prioritizing virtue, self-knowledge, goodness, truth, and happiness over wealth, fame, and power; he developed explanations of ethics, believing that evil is always done out of ignorance and harms the doer more than the victim; he defined concepts of the soul; and the list goes on. What is most notable, however, is that, in contrast to the more cosmic focus of the Presocratic thinkers, Socrates maintained that the purpose of philosophy was to answer the very practical, down-to-earth question "What is the way we ought to live?"

Despite his good intentions, Socrates' efforts were often poorly received by the public. After pushing his luck too far, he was put on trial for religious impiety and corrupting the youth. He was found guilty and sentenced to death. In 399 BC, he would be given a cup of poison hemlock to drink, which would slowly move through his body until reaching his heart and taking from Socrates his last breath—one of history's greatest minds shut down for asking too many questions about a world that was not yet ready to admit it was still at the starting line. Although his mission would be cut short, it would be far from unsuccessful.

One of Socrates' greatest legacies was his student Plato, who would successfully take the handoff from him and officially begin the relay race of Western philosophy.

Plato would follow in Socrates' footsteps of skepticism, critical questioning, reasoning, and the prioritization of knowledge toward achieving what was termed *arete*, or virtue. Unlike Socrates, however, Plato wrote down his work and crafted a more defined philosophical system, producing thirty-six books during his lifetime and setting up the first ever university, which was called the Academy. It is for this reason that Plato is considered by many to be the first ever true philosopher, at least in the Western tradition. In his work, Plato would explore love, friendship, beauty, politics, ethics, and happiness. However, arguably one of his most prominent and influential philosophical contributions was his thinking about thinking itself. Following Socrates' tradition of skepticism, Plato's next move was to question how we can and do come to know things at all. Ultimately, Plato believed that knowledge is possible and that there are fixed, objective truths to be discovered and used—or more accurately, rediscovered, because Plato believed all knowledge was innate prior to birth and then forgotten upon birth, requiring recollection through reasoning. In what would become known as Platonic idealism, Plato would separate the realm of truth from the material world, distinguishing the world of things as we perceive them from the world of things as they really are. For Plato, reality as we observe it is a flawed reflection of a higher truth that exists in a realm beyond time, space, and the human mind, containing universalities and abstract objects that exist in their most pure, unchanging ideal form. Plato would refer to these as the *Forms* and suggested that they function as the fundamental building blocks of the material world. As a simplified example, consider how there are many trees in the world but that no two trees are identical. Despite the fact that each tree is different from the rest, all of them—despite their differences—are still trees. According to Plato, this is because all trees are imperfect shadows of the perfect, ideal Form of a tree—that all trees have as their model. It is through our knowledge of this perfect and ideal Form of a tree that we recognize a tree as a tree; that we discern the *treeness* in every tree. From a practical standpoint, Plato suggested that through reason and philosophy, individuals and societies could understand ideals such as justice, happiness, friendship, being, and goodness, in order strive toward and attain them.

Plato would illustrate this theory with his most popular metaphor, the *Allegory of the Cave*, which is contained in book seven of his work, *The Republic*. In this allegory, he tells the story of a group of prisoners who have been chained up facing a wall inside a cave. They have been there ever since birth and have no knowledge of the outside world. On the wall that they are facing, shadows of different shapes are cast by people passing in front of a fire behind them with various objects. The prisoners name and classify the shadows, believing that they are seeing the true forms of things. However, when suddenly one of the prisoners is freed, he exits the cave and discovers the real world outside—all the actual forms and qualities of the objects that were previously just displayed as shadows to him. This prisoner, after realizing what he has become aware of, returns to the cave to tell the other prisoners. However, when he does, they think he has gone insane or been brainwashed or corrupted by whatever is outside. They respond not only with resistance but also violence, hostile to his attempt to challenge their beliefs and encourage a new, improved knowledge of the world.

There are, of course, multiple ways of interpreting this allegory, but in the context of his theory of Forms, Plato creates the distinction between the shadows and the objects they are cast by to parallel the Forms and the material world we experience—how we are all caved inside our own senses, restricted from and ignorant of the true forms of things. The escaped prisoner, of course, represents the philosopher who, through reason, righteously tries to communicate his discoveries but is resisted or even killed by the public.

As interesting, innovative, and useful as this allegory is, there is at least one obvious issue with it, which is perhaps mirrored in the problem of Plato's philosophy and almost all of Western philosophy as a whole. How does the prisoner who was freed know that once outside, he is not merely in another sort of cave? How does he know that the objects in their supposed truer, pure form outside the cave are not merely another sort of crude shadow cast by another purer source he is not yet aware of or perhaps can never be aware of? And if he were to somehow reach or discover a subsequent truer realm, how would he know this one to be true? Does not the increasingly common discovery of 'obviously' true things to be untrue increase the odds that what is currently being discovered is also untrue?

Of course, although Socrates and Plato were fundamental to the founding of Western philosophy, both combining to influence essential ideas and questions about reality, knowledge, reason, and the way an individual and society ought to exist, much of what they believed and claimed does not hold up today. Although perhaps they were the escaped prisoners of their time, they were nonetheless still prisoners in another cave just outside of the first one. Perhaps all reality is a prison and time is its guard.

In Plato's *Apology*, Socrates says to the citizens of Athens following his trial, "I prophesy to you that after my death the punishment will soon descend upon you, a punishment far more severe than that which you have inflicted on me. You will have caused my death, hoping in vain to escape from my critical questioning . . ." Around 2,400 years later, it would seem that Socrates' prophecy, in at least some sense, has come true. We have yet to escape from his critical questioning. With each new generation, each new philosophy, and each new realm of knowledge, we find ourselves in the wake of Socrates, still either unsure or in denial. Socrates and Plato gave us some of the first tools needed to begin taking the whole world apart, but they never had, and we likely never will have, an instruction manual to put it back together. We still know very little of what it means to be a self, let alone a true self, what it means to live or how we ought to, what consciousness is, why there is life or a universe at all, what the ultimate purpose of literally anything and everything is, if there is any truth and how we can know for sure, and the list goes on. One of the only true constants that appears to have remained from the early groundwork of ancient Greek philosophy is perhaps the recognition of our ignorance, the Socratic paradox: *I know that I know nothing.* Socrates knew he knew nothing but seemed to believe that this paradox could be overcome to good end. Perhaps it can; certainly in many practical cases, it seems to be. But in the case of the fundamental questions about existence, identity, meaning, and ethics, perhaps philosophy is, in some sense, futile. Perhaps there are no ultimate answers in philosophy, perhaps there never will be, but there are no ultimate answers in music, in art, in a beautiful landscape, or in a conversation with a friend, and yet, I know of no one who does not find value, insight, love, and solace in all of these things.

Perhaps by means of the very same thing that cursed humanity with the need to philosophize, we can learn, through philosophy, to enjoy philosophy's futility. Perhaps the purpose of philosophy, then—at least of a certain broader kind—is best recontextualized so that the ambiguity and unknowingness becomes, rather than a means, an end in and of itself. Perhaps what we should and only can do is to try to enjoy the process of playing with the blocks of philosophy like children playing with toy blocks for no reason other than the curiosity and fun of it; not because in the end the blocks will provide something that stays up forever, but because we inevitably will take the blocks down, put them away for a little while, and then play with them again on another day, in a different way. And for that, whether or not we agree with Socrates, Plato, or the Western philosophical tradition in general, we should thank them for this—for providing the tools of thinking and questioning that have allowed and will continue to allow for the development of philosophical wonder.

TAOISM & THE ART OF FLOWING WITH LIFE

The Philosophy of Lao Tzu

Everything is pushed or pulled through something by something toward something. All that exists is created and moved by some substrate force, evolving from this to that, toward apparent nothing for apparently no reason other than itself. What is this movement? What is our role within it? And can we integrate more seamlessly into it?

The ancient Chinese philosophy known as Taoism is one of the primary schools of thought that emerged and sustained out of a volatile but intellectually enriched period of Chinese history, roughly between 700 and 200 BC. Its origins, longstanding popularity, and viewpoints are often similar and discussed in relation to other leading Eastern philosophies like Buddhism and Confucianism. By coincidence, Taoism can also be said to contain many similarities to the ancient Greek and Roman philosophy of Stoicism, although the two schools did not come in contact when they first formed. It is generally accepted that Taoism was founded by the writer and philosopher known as Lao Tzu, who is credited with authoring the foundational Taoist text, the *Tao Te Ching*. However, there is no substantiated proof that Lao Tzu ever actually existed, and some historians believe that the name could merely be a contrivance of sorts, either intentionally or unintentionally creating a figure of legend for the school. This, however, is also unproven. If Lao Tzu was real, he is believed to have been a record keeper in the court of Zhou in around fifth-century BC China. At some point during his later life, the story goes that Lao Tzu grew tired of the increasing bureaucracy and corruption of Zhou and decided to leave. On his way out of the kingdom, a border official recognized him and, knowing of his reputation of wisdom, asked Lao Tzu if he would write down his insights prior to leaving. Allegedly, Lao Tzu did, and this would become the *Tao Te Ching*, the most translated philosophical or religious book in all of history, after the bible.

There are, like most things of this sort, different forms and sects of Taoism that follow different ways of behaving and thinking. As a result of its inherently vague and somewhat open-ended nature, a variety of philosophical, religious, and political interpretations have formed and fragmented over time. Thus, Taoism has been made into somewhat of a broad, malleable philosophy. What is generally considered Taoism today, specifically in the modern West, naturally deviates, at least to some extent, from the initial thinking. Separated by upwards of 2,500 years of time and a globe of space, this is to be expected, but it is worth noting and respecting. Ironically, though, the possible fluctuation and evolution of Taoism is perhaps a testament to one of its own primary ideas. Central to Taoism is the idea that everything is in a continual state of flux, ceaselessly changing and adapting. Thus, no single idea or thing is to be attached to. Nothing is to be forced in or out of place. All is to be permitted to run its natural course, subject to the one, constant, unchanging truth: everything changes. And so, it is perhaps nothing but a confirmation of this idea that the interpretation of Taoism's ideas, in some sense, changes over time.

To understand the philosophical basis of Taoist ideas, it is essential to understand the concept known as *The Tao*. The Tao is generally translated as *the way*, which in the context of Taoism, refers to the natural way or order of the universe. Although, the Tao is more of a blanket, abstract term for what is beyond human conception and comprehension—a sort of force or substrate that creates and propels all things for apparently no reason; the incomprehensible origin and destination of the universe where logic and human sensibility collapse; the infinite and the nothing in a singular, unified, eternal dance with themselves for themselves; a creation without a creator. However, according to Lao Tzu, even here, this kind of explanation still misses the point and essence of the Tao. "The Tao that can be told is not the eternal Tao.

The name that can be named is not the eternal name. The unnamable is the eternal real," Lao Tzu wrote in the opening lines of the *Tao Te Ching*. The Tao is, or at least appears, paradoxical in this sense. It is a word that is spoken and a concept that is, in a roundabout way, understood, yet it declares itself beyond conceptual understanding and states that it cannot be stated. However, perhaps it is the case that sometimes words and concepts of this form can work like fingers, pointing in the direction of a *thing* that can only truly be seen and understood by living it.

Essential to Taoism is living according to the Tao. Put more simply, it is living in accordance with nature. Lao Tzu suggests that one can accomplish this by accepting the fluctuation of everything and giving up rigid judgments, attachments, expectations, and our efforts to control our lives. In doing so, one becomes more closely intertwined with the natural order of things, taking on a sort of fluid, intuitive, and harmonious relationship with the natural world. Perhaps one of Taoism's most useful and slightly more practical ideas that stems from this is the concept of *Wu Wei*, which generally translates as non-doing or effortless action. This idea does not literally suggest doing nothing or doing things that are easy, but rather, it suggests cultivating abilities, circumstances, and a lifestyle in which one frequently becomes fully immersed in one's actions—so much so that we are almost carried by our actions, rather than the other way around. In other words, engaging in tasks with a deep focus and presence, surrendering to more spontaneous instincts. In the same way that a bowl's emptiness allows for it to be filled and made useful, for Lao Tzu, emptying or stilling the mind allows actions to unfold more effectively. In many respects, this idea of Wu Wei parallels modern day positive psychology's notion of the flow state. They differ, of course, in that the latter is underpinned by science and the former by more spiritualized philosophy, but at bottom, both seem to point to the same relative idea—a state where one experiences a deep focus, satisfaction, natural efficiency, and the absence of self-consciousness. One might experience this state when they are in the thrall of a creative flurry, and a work of art seems to almost create itself; or a moment in a sport where one seems to almost know exactly what to do, two moves ahead, without ever stopping and thinking; or when one comes up with an idea or the right thing to say as soon as they stop trying to come up with it; or perhaps the more general gut instincts and intuitions felt in everyday life that seem to just feel right for no other reason, and are.

For Lao Tzu, life broadly is to be lived in this zone. Like how the breath breathes, the heart beats, the birds fly, the fish migrate, the wind blows, the earth spins—all perfectly on their own—the Taoists believe that life operates most functionally when simplified to a more intuitive, natural intelligence. Like water is humble and soft yet erodes the sides of mountains and dissolves rocks by quietly, patiently, and persistently flowing its natural course, so too should the human act. Lao Tzu wrote:

> Can you coax your mind from its wandering and keep to the original oneness? . . . Can you cleanse your inner vision until you see nothing but the light? Can you love people and lead them without imposing your will? Can you deal with the most vital matters by letting events take their course? Can you step back from your own mind and thus, understand all things? . . . This is the supreme virtue.

We are drawn to the graceful yet indifferent quality of nature. When we see someone forcing something, be it an artistic performance or a performance of the *self* in everyday, ordinary life, we almost always know when it is fraudulent, and we almost always dislike it. We say that it doesn't feel natural, that it feels forced, that someone is being fake. We have a seemingly innate sensitivity to what is tried rather than simply done. Ultimately, we want truth. We want honesty. We want the natural motion of everything—some thing or essence that cannot be explained by anything else other than the act of doing or experiencing it. Words and ideas of the intellect seem to fall short of the apparent deeper truth that is revealed by this authentic poetry in motion.

Realistically, this notion of not trying and relinquishing conscious effort is perhaps practical and effective in cases of artistic, athletic, and certain social circumstances, but in the broader application of the idea, it isn't obvious how much one really should, or even can, let go and accept the way things are. Can the can of worms of intellectualization, force, and desire truly be closed once it has already been opened? Moreover, is it not possible that conscious effort, force-fulness, and opposing action with the apparent natural world are all in fact natural parts of the natural world? In the context of Taoism, could working against the Tao merely be the Tao working against the Tao for the sake of its perpetuation? Perhaps a further step in the logical path of Taoism, and philosophies like it, involves an even greater surrender that doesn't even permit one to choose or consider if they are surrender-ing or not. Rather, one is born into the surrender. If, in Taoism, the relationship of all things is a cooperative, unified whole, even when things appear in conflict, are 'human' and 'nature' not always in cooperation, even when they seem to oppose each other? If dark-ness creates light, silence creates sound, beauty creates ugliness, good creates bad, does forcefulness not create non-forcefulness? Does man not create nature? Does consciousness not create unconsciousness? 'Human' is part and parcel of nature, and so, how could humans act in any other way? How could manmade material or action ever not be natural?

Of course, this is just one counter idea that stems from just one interpretation of an elusive, mysterious Taoist idea. And to step back a little, there is no ques-tion that our conscious observations and seemingly logical conclusions do often fool us, and we are, in many cases, clearly deviating from what's best when we force or strive for what we think is. Perhaps the remaining questions are: when should we and when shouldn't we? And how does one find out without screwing the whole thing up? Perhaps these questions miss the point. Perhaps the point ignores these questions.

Of course, like all ideals of philosophy or religion, Taoism's concepts are likely just that: ideals that are not without some level of contradiction or general incompleteness on their own. But regardless of this and the potential limits of its applicability, the concepts suggested by Taoism are filled with rich insights that provide worthy, useful counterweights to the more common, brutish ways of mind and culture that make us think that things must always be a different way or must go one's own way for it to be the right way, that there must always be some better ideal around the corner that isn't or couldn't be in this moment right now, and that one needs to seek or strive for what they already have and know.

THE ART OF LETTING GO

The Philosophy of the Buddha

What does it mean to live well and be virtuous in a world of suffering, chaos, and deterioration? What does it mean to go on living in a consciousness that is inevitably bound to the struggle of becoming more confused and tormented as it becomes more capable and aware? Generally speaking, most religious and philosophical concepts are spurred out of these sorts of challenges and questions. They represent humanity's attempt to overcome or deal with the deficiencies and difficulties forced into each pair of unrequested human hands. One perhaps especially unique example of such an attempt is the philosophy and religion of Buddhism.

Somewhere between the sixth and fourth centuries BC, in what is now Southern Nepal, a boy named Siddhartha Gautama was born. He was born to an aristocratic family, his father, Śuddhodana, being the king of a growing state on the Indian subcontinent. When Siddhartha was born, a holy messenger prophesied that he would become one of two things: a great king or a great religious leader. When his father received this prophecy, being the conservative king he was, he determined that he would ensure that Siddhartha would become the former. He would ensure this by completely sheltering Siddhartha, confining him within a massive palace he had walled off from the rest of the world, rigidly filtering what was allowed in by a standard of perfect health, beauty, and luxury, constantly cleansing the palace of any signs of imperfection, discomfort, misery, ugliness, illness, and death, preventing Siddhartha from ever knowing that they existed. All of this, in Śuddhodana's mind, was to create a world that would be easy for Siddhartha to fall in love with and desire kingship of, removing any need to consider, question, or become interested in religious or spiritual domains.

Throughout his childhood and into early adulthood, however, Siddhartha would, for this very reason, become increasingly curious about his conception of the world. At twenty-nine years old, his existential curiosity finally boiled over the walls of the palace and into the unknown and prohibited kingdom beyond.

At this point, Siddhartha would make the decision to take his first journey out of the palace and into the world. In anticipation of this, in order to maintain the masquerade of a perfect, redeemable world, his father ordered the streets to be removed of all signs of pain, suffering, sickness, old age, and death. Despite this, however, while being taken through the city on a chariot, Siddhartha would pass by an extremely sick man, his body clearly blemished and written on by the conditions of his ailment. When Siddhartha saw this, he asked the chariot driver who was escorting him what was wrong with the man. The chariot driver informed Siddhartha that the man was sick and explained to him what this meant.

On a second journey outside the palace, Siddhartha would next be exposed to an elderly man who looked extremely feeble, frail, and wrinkled. Again, when he saw this, having never seen a person of such an age, he asked the driver what was wrong. The driver informed him of the phenomenon of aging and how, like that man, all human bodies grow old with time, decaying, and becoming unattractive and weak.

On his third journey outside the palace, this time, Siddhartha would encounter a funeral procession passing through the streets, exposing him for the first time to a dead body. Again, Siddhartha asked what was wrong and was informed by the driver about death and the inevitable finite limit of all living things.

Now, completely and utterly devastated by his collection of newfound insights into the fragility of the physical body, the temporal horizon of age, and the finite, terminal nature of existence, of which all living things, including himself, would inevitably face, he felt the final straw break, shattering his comfortable, sheltered, youthful image of the world and replacing it with its exposed, horrifying one. Realizing this truth of the world, now, Siddhartha could no longer stay in the palace. Rather, he found himself compelled by a quest to overcome and deal with his new conception of life.

On a fourth journey outside the palace, Siddhartha, now seeking answers, noticed a meditating holy man in the city who seemed to be at complete peace amidst the horrors that surrounded him. Curious about the man's apparent ability to attain such a state, Siddhartha would become inspired and spend the following months on a sort of spiritual quest, seeking holy practices, ideas, and answers. However, being a very pragmatic and inquisitive man by this point, refusing to mindlessly agree with the conventions, orthodoxies, and blind faiths required by many of the religious ideas and practices of the time, Siddhartha found himself at the very brink of available ideologies and methods, yet still completely unsatisfied.

At some point, with a group of several other men, Siddhartha would engage in the extreme, radical spiritual practice known as asceticism, which involves a complete renunciation of earthly indulgences and pleasures in an attempt to loosen the attachment of the body to the physical world, and in doing so, free the *self*. After many months of starving himself into an unrecognizably weak, malnourished, and skin-draped collection of bones, Siddhartha still had found nothing in the form of a resolution or answer. He could not think straight, and the extreme physical deprivation only created more futile suffering. And so, he began to eat food again, returning to somewhere in the middle of the two extremes.

Now, ostracized by the ascetic men for what they felt was giving up, Siddhartha would continue on his own, meditating alone in the forest away from the rest of the world. He would continue to both eat and meditate, not depriving his body nor pursuing much beyond what his body needed for basic comfort. Throughout this period, Siddhartha would experience a collection of introspective realizations. It was here that Siddhartha would begin to formulate his fundamental philosophical tenets, and it was here that Siddhartha's story would become the story of the Buddha, or 'the enlightened one.' In this moment, Buddhism would begin its journey in human history, challenging and changing the course of religious, social, and philosophical orthodoxy forever.

It isn't clear how much literal truth is contained in the story of the Buddha. Most of what is known about the Buddha and his teachings is based on oral accounts that were written down centuries after his death, leaving plenty of room for various interpretations and supplementary details to be added and twisted. Furthermore, there are numerous versions of his story that are accepted as accurate, each with at least slightly different details, tones, spiritual references, and overarching implications. However, regardless of literal accuracy and variation, the general story of the Buddha arguably always remains the same at its core: it is a story of us all. It is the story of growing up, becoming curious and tempted, seeking to move out and beyond the borders of the sheltered reality maintained by our parents, society, and our underdeveloped psyche, beginning to discover life's contaminated horrors for the first time, and the extreme lengths we often go to in order to try to understand, overcome, and escape them.

In terms of the Buddha's specific philosophical ideas, his core principles are contained in what he termed *The Four Noble Truths*. The First Noble Truth is that life is fundamentally suffering. No matter who or what they are, all living things are bound and connected by this intrinsic existential quality of suffering, in its broadest sense. The Second Noble Truth argues that this suffering is a consequence of our desires and attachments. The third truth, in a revolutionary way of thinking for its time, goes on to claim that since suffering is a product of attachment and desire, one can personally overcome and end suffering by eliminating or recalibrating one's desires and attachments. The fourth and final Noble Truth contains the steps Buddha believed were necessary to do so. This collection of steps would be named the *Noble Eightfold Path*, also often referred to as the *Middle Way*. These eight steps include right view, right intention, right speech, right action, right livelihood, right effort, right mindfulness, and right concentration. These concepts are not so much steps to be achieved or discovered in a linear order, but rather, a wheel of actively circulating behaviors and wisdom that one must constantly turn. In broad summary, it essentially calls for the practice of wisdom, universal compassion, moderation, self-knowledge, and reaching enlightenment, or Nirvana, through non-attachment and the elimination of desire. Essential to the success of the Buddha's teachings is this final idea of non-attachment or no desire. Admittedly, this concept can sound rather counterintuitive at first, but it starts by recognizing the true nature of the self, which is, in at least one interpretation of the Buddha's teachings, non-self (or emptiness). Buddha argued that our external world is in perpetual, unattainable flux, and consequently, so too are we. We are but collections of constantly changing interactions between the world and our thoughts, and thus, the idea of a fixed, independent, identifiable *self* is a delusion. This is essential to understand because it suggests that the *self* that we are trying to satisfy, escape, or eternalize never even really exists in the first place. Rather, the capital *I* that we describe is merely a state of emptiness constantly being filled and emptied by the succession of each moment. This concept can perhaps be experienced distinctly when one considers how there is no real central point of sensation and experience when one experiences something like smell, mental vision, memory, or emotion. Of course, they can be pointed to the mind, but where in the mind? After the nose, who or what is smelling? Or, let's say, if you imagined a purple cat right now and visualized it in your head, where is the purple cat? How is the purple cat? Where are you seeing it from? There is just a blank emptiness filled up by the interacting thoughts and sensations of the moment, all becoming one constantly changing hybrid of *self* and material world.

Buddha's teachings are about reorienting our view of our *self* so that we see that there is no *self*, and then reorient our view of the world. According to the Buddha, we suffer not as a result of not having enough things like money, status, success, or ideal external circumstances, but because the desire for such things is attached to the impossible delusion of a permanent *self* capable of being satisfied by desire. And the only way out of this is ending, or at least attempting to reduce, one's dependence on such desires and attachments, living with some form of restrained moderation, and conquering the prodding delusion of *self*. According to the Buddha:

> Though one may conquer a thousand times a thousand men in battle, yet he indeed is the noblest victor who conquers himself. Self-conquest is far better than the conquest of others. Not even a god, an angel, Mara or Brahma can turn into defeat the victory of a person who is self-subdued and ever restrained in conduct.

Of course, Buddhism is not without its shortcomings and outdated artifacts. For secular types, its religious association can likely pose its fair share of problems. And outside of this, just in terms of its general, core principle, can one truly desire no desire? Does this work as a final desire, ending the very thing required to enact it? Or, does it create a mirage that holds us in further submission to desire? Moreover, to what extent do we really have any control over our desires, the information we encounter, and how it all works together to affect us? And as the world and humanity continue to develop further and further, and temptations and indulgences and distractions seep into every pore of modern societal life, we are likely left with an extremely difficult uphill climb into even the secular form of the Buddha's teachings.

However, regardless of this and any other difficulties or pitfalls, Buddhism remains a highly unique and compelling system of thinking. Over millennia, it has seen many different iterations, interpretations, updates, and effects, not only in the East, but also in the West, even influencing many significant Western philosophers such as Arthur Schopenhauer, Friedrich Nietzsche, Ralph Waldo Emerson, Emil Cioran, Alan Watts, and many others. Currently, it is the world's fourth largest religion, with over half a billion followers worldwide, primarily divided into two main overarching schools: Theravada and Mahayana. At its core, Buddhism is one of the most unique and dynamic schools of religious thought, grounding its ideas in empirical experience and practical methodologies, making its wisdom accessible without necessarily depending on gods or faith in the unknowable and untouchable, bringing the spiritual down into the hands of the pragmatic, everyday person. Perhaps most significantly, it confronts the suffering and darkness of life directly and does not keep us in the palace of ignorance. It does not try to lie to us. It does not shelter or coddle. It makes its best efforts to thread the needle between the minimums and maximums of life and lead us down a path toward some semblance of hope in living well in spite of what's really out there.

THE ZEN RIDDLES NO ONE CAN ANSWER

Amonk seeking guidance from Zhao Zhou, the master of a Zen monastery, asks Zhao Zhou if he will teach him the way to enlightenment.

Zhao Zhou answers the monk, "Have you eaten your meal?"

The monk replies, "Yes, I have."

"Then go wash your bowl," says Zhao Zhou.

At that moment, the monk was enlightened.

Right off the bat, you might find this dialogue to be abrupt and confusing. With further thought, you might try to figure out why—what the meal and the bowl might represent and what the metaphorical lesson might be. After more thought, you might conclude that it all appears to have no point. With this, you would be correct. It doesn't. However, in this discovery, you would have realized the point, because the point is to not have one. So, technically, you would have also been wrong. You might find this completely contradictory and foolish. Again, you would be correct. This is also the point.

With only a little dissection, this simple, seemingly pointless riddle reveals itself to be a whirlwind of regressive contradictions and confusions when put through the analytical mind. How can it have a point by not having one? How can it mean anything by not meaning anything? How can one argue for and against it at the same time? This paradoxical and brain-breaking riddle is known as a kōan. A kōan is a riddle or dialectic meditation device used in Zen Buddhist practice that is intentionally designed to, at least on the surface, be unclear and obscure. Its point is not to provide a conclusion or answer to the question presented, but rather, to disregard the relevance of the answer—to detach itself from the functions of conclusion and singular resolution. There are over a thousand known kōans that follow this format, all used to test and challenge Zen Buddhists and reveal the obscurity and limits of the mind.

In general, life is uncertain, confusing, and paradoxical. As hard as we work against this, it mostly remains so. No matter our efforts, every time we believe we have some understanding or control over life, like water in the palm of the hand, the tighter we squeeze, the more it eludes our grip. Sciences, religions, and philosophies make sense of the world through various methods (some more successfully than others), but nonetheless, all of them face inevitable limits: the human mind and the time in which they are devised.

By sheer lack of alternatives, we understand the world with thoughts and words. Through them, we can create systems of order and understanding like logic, story, and social structure. This aptitude is fundamental to our ability to survive, coexist, communicate, deal with physical objects, and so on. However, thoughts and words, of course, can only describe and understand the world in terms of thoughts and words. As a result, they cannot make sense of what exists beyond thoughts and words, which so much of life does. Like any tools, thinking and language are limited to the confines of their abilities. Like a hammer cannot screw in a screw, and a nail cannot cut a board of wood, the human mind cannot make sense of the mindless. A hammer can perhaps smash a screw in, and nail can perhaps split a board of wood, just like the mind can perhaps consider life, but none of these items or tools fully suit the jobs that they are carrying out here, and thus, will fall short in properly completing them. A kōan embodies this notion. As opposed to most stories, ideas, and answers that attempt to fight against the concepts of obscurity and absurdity in life by using defined structure, logic, and resolutions, the kōan harmonizes with the obscurity of life and disregards the need for conclusive answers. In rough terms, Zen Buddhism, in general, is founded on this synchronization with the obscure and abstract. To put it in a more specific context, Zen is a subset of Buddhism that is not concerned with concrete ideas and concepts, and so, it is not really much of a belief system at all. Rather, it is considered to be more of a state of being. In other words, it involves living in accordance with one's limitations to articulate and understand things in any absolute sense and living more off intuition and spontaneity. Paradoxically, in the attempt to define Zen, you have already incorrectly defined it. Alan Watts said that "Zen is trying to point to the physical universe so that you can look at it without forming ideas about it." Instead of saying life is this or that, Zen says life is unclear and always changing, at least in terms of words and ideas. This is to say that the universe is not to be packaged or structured in some human or rational way, but rather, it is to be experienced from the perspective of a passenger, flowing with it, and avoiding attachment to things within it that might make one stuck or rigid. It's as if we are all swimming or floating down a river in which there are rocks that protrude out of the river's surface. These rocks represent various things and ideas that might be appealing or seem reasonable to grab a hold of and stop ourselves from going further downriver. However, if we stop to hold onto a rock, we stop moving. The water continues to flow beneath us, but we remain stuck and rigid. Zen suggests that in this, we will begin to experience an increasing pain and suffering that arises from being attached to something and disconnected from the fluid movement of activity happening around us.

At the risk of adding further confusion and paradox to an already confusing and paradoxical thought experiment, a kōan does not appear to suggest that we should cease asking questions or thinking about the answers to questions or anything of that sort. Kōans did not spring up out of lack of thought or contemplation, but rather, out of a specific sort of contemplation: a self-referential thinking that denies its ability to be a single, concrete, and universal thought that answers or understands what might exist beyond itself. Zen and the lesson of the kōans suggest that we should flow with life, ask questions, contemplate them, but not become tricked by any singular idea or answer that might tempt us into a final resolution. This is, of course, extremely difficult, especially since we tend to extract our identities out of our beliefs and ideas, and thus, our minds work very hard to hold onto them. Arguably, it is unlikely that we will ever be able to fully avoid being tricked by this function of the mind and ego. Even holding onto the idea of not holding onto any ideas is in fact holding onto an idea. However, perhaps by considering the lesson of the kōans, the more practical point is to help remind us of the playfulness of most things, see through the contrived, take ourselves a little less seriously, and open ourselves up to the likely paradox of all the ideas, experiences, and people we encounter. Just like how the center of a tornado is calm with little to no motion, despite it being surrounded by a coil of rapid, violent wind, we can live in the center of the tornado of knowing and unknowing and still remain calm and at ease.

THE FREEDOM OF BEING NOBODY

One of mankind's greatest longings is complete freedom. One of mankind's greatest limitations is the inability to ever truly be free.

We want the frictionless state of our origins. We want the autonomy of a god. We want the sea of reality to part at the whim of our fluctuating, individual will. We want, as is so often the case, what we cannot have.

Of course, there are many different types of freedom, and there are many layers and nuances within each type, but arguably, absolute freedom of the existential kind, in which one is able to do, feel, and choose what one wants, how and when they see fit without any kind of coercion, restraint, or imposition, is the ideal of freedom that drives the passionate pursuit of all other kinds, and perhaps, all human activity in general. However, in the final analysis, this ultimate endgame of freedom appears to be an incoherent impossibility. At the top of the pyramid of freedom, even an individual who is lucky enough to have unfastened all material and societal shackles remains unfree, restricted and told what to do, when to do it, and why to do it.

This individual, of course possessing one of the most basic freedoms, physical freedom, can move their body around the world as they please. But in just this first layer of analysis, obvious restrictions are found. Of course, they can only move according to how their body does and can, and they can only move through and with the body. We generally do not see the body as a ball and chain because we associate part of who we are with it and only know of existence through it, but it takes no more than a sick stomach or migraine to realize just how heavy this corporeal weight is, how stricken and limited by it we are. We are stuck inside the body, captives to it, subject to its faulty and fragile mechanisms that do and will break, keeping us bound in space according to its condition—until it finally turns itself off, and us with it. And what's more, our body controls much of what we choose to do with it— how we move it, where we move it, and why. Being told when to eat, when to go to the bathroom, when to sleep, when to wake up; that is the daily routine of a prisoner, not a free human being.

Of course, one can decide to temporarily resist their bodily urges and not eat, sleep, and so forth, momentarily experiencing a fleeting distinction between mind and body. But it takes very little time for the conspiracy between the mind and body to reveal itself. The mental sensations that are a corollary of the body's state will soon compel the individual to behave accordingly, and get in line. This, of course, is just a physical issue, though. Psychologically, the individual is able to think and consider everything beyond the mere urges and physical conditions of their body and environment. This much is true, but is our relationship with the mind in the realm of thought not ultimately the same as our physical relationship with the body? We can only think through the mind, and we can only think in the way our mind thinks. We are given one lens through which to see the world, with one type of software running on one type of hardware to process all that we intake and experience. If an artist was commissioned for a job and told that they were free to make anything they wanted—as long as they produce it using an etch-a-sketch—would they really be free to make anything they wanted? Only in some sense. In truth, the freest of people are free to think and see things however they choose, but only so long as it is with words that exist through concepts that have been construed in a brain that has been built with respect to an environment that has been experienced, all moved by the laws of the natural world.

Our mind's abilities are its constraints, and its constraints inform us what to think and see, each condition of the brain working in relation to the world like levees and dams controlling the flow of thought, each thought emerging out of the cause-and-effect ripples on the surface of its unending self-orchestrated flow.

We are caught in this movement, swept away uncontrollably without ever choosing where we started from or where we are going. Being compelled what to think and how to see is the life of an indoctrinated person, not a free human being.

It is a demonstration of humanity's overzealous ego and anthropocentrism to think that so long as no other humans tell them what to do, they are free.

Human beings should undoubtedly strive and fight for all their earthly freedoms within the physical, social, economic, and political domains of the world. But if and once they have, the remaining unsatisfied existential freedom, in search of which they will continue to drink and run and lust and love, perhaps requires a different kind of consideration. "Freedom can be manifested only in the void of beliefs, in the absence of axioms, and only where the laws have no more authority than a hypothesis," wrote the philosopher Emil Cioran.

The closest thing to absolute existential freedom, it seems, is freedom from freedom itself—freedom from the constraints that the concept of freedom imposes. Being totally existentially free or unfree implies being a defined, separate thing that can be contained by some other thing. In a letter of condolence to a grieving father, Albert Einstein wrote:

> A human being is a part of the whole, called by us "Universe," a part limited in time and space. He experiences himself, his thoughts and feelings as something separate from the rest—a kind of optical delusion of his

consciousness. The striving to free oneself from this delusion is the one issue of true [religiosity]. Not to nourish it but to try to overcome it is the way to reach the attainable measure of peace of mind.

Most would likely agree with the premise that the individual is essentially associated with their brain. But if so, which part of the brain, which area, which spot? Can you find it? Can you feel it? Can you locate it when you close your eyes or point to it if you took a brain scan? No. Consciousness is who we are—how we identify ourselves through experience. But consciousness is, when distilled down empirically, a strange, empty awareness, malleably undefined and inexorably connected with everything that makes and interacts with it (and doesn't). You are not the master of your mind. You are not the servant. You are both and neither. You are your thoughts and the lineage of every bit of history that they touched to get to you. You are the words you are reading and the mind that is automatically processing them. You are the mind that will forget them in some amount of time. You are everything you've heard and perceived. You are everything you've never heard or perceived. You are everything you've ever hated. You are everything you've ever loved. You are what's inside and what's outside your mind and your body. And you are none of the above. If you exist, you cannot be free. If there is no you, you cannot be contained by anything.

Like the desire for perfect, unending happiness, the desire for complete and absolute freedom is impossible. But like happiness, it is, in its true, ultimate form, a state that comes and goes, unattainable in the ideal but attainable in the moment—in the moments when we surrender to the complete unified image of being, when we cease trying to square circles and placate everything that contests us, when we stop trying to escape what cannot be escaped. It is the classic lesson: the Chinese finger trap, the Tao in Taoism, Nirvana in Buddhism, the silence of Wittgenstein; the harder one tries, the harder one flails, the more entrenched one becomes. In the words of Kahlil Gibran, from his poem, *On Freedom*:

At the city gate and by your fireside I have seen you prostrate yourself and worship your own freedom,

Even as slaves humble themselves before a tyrant and praise him though he slays them.

Ay, in the grove of the temple and in the shadow of the citadel I have seen the freest among you wear their freedom as a yoke and a handcuff.

And my heart bled within me; for you can only be free when even the desire of seeking freedom becomes a harness to you, and when you cease to speak of freedom as a goal and a fulfilment.

. . .

In truth that which you call freedom is the strongest of these chains, though its links glitter in the sun and dazzle your eyes.

STOICISM & THE ART
OF NOT CARING

We are born into this world hungry, vulnerable, and confused. As we go through life, we attempt to eliminate these feelings by trying to control the conditions of the world around us. We seek to accomplish and obtain things, achieve higher status, acquire wealth or fame, develop power, and so on. We live with a persisting hopefulness that, in the future, we will have and control enough to free ourselves of our desire, vulnerability, and confusion. This hopeful vision of the future might sound reasonable, but perhaps it is what keeps us with our problems.

Stoicism is a philosophy that started in ancient Greece, and was then further popularized in ancient Rome. Stoicism is an especially unique philosophy in how potently it has withstood the test of time over thousands of years. The teachings and wisdom of Stoic philosophy are equally relevant today, if not more so. In recent history, Stoicism has found huge appeal. It was used and advocated for by Nelson

Mandela, written about by popular modern authors like Tim Ferris, Robert Greene, and Ryan Holiday, just to name a few, and has found a large community on the internet. Stoicism's enduring popularity is not without good reason. The principles of Stoicism can help us find calmness, presence, and resilience in a world of increasingly overt chaos, anxiety, and the insatiable desire for more.

In the Stoic view, we exist in a reality that does not care about our opinion of it. We cannot ask it nicely to remove the chaos, suffering, hardship, and uncertainty, nor can we will ourselves onto it with force in order to do so. However, Stoicism does not suggest that we are helpless victims of the world. Rather, Stoicism claims that there are two domains of life: the external—the things outside of our mind, which we cannot control—and the internal—our mental reactions and interpretations of the external, which we can control. When we persist with the belief that things outside of ourselves or things in the future will provide us with a form of ultimate happiness, we exchange the real moments of our lives for ones that do not exist. We become dependent on things outside of ourselves that we cannot control, and we endlessly run on a treadmill of unceasing desire.

We can and should engage our nature to progress and pursue bigger, faster, better, and more interesting things, but we should ensure that in our pursuits, we are intentional about what we are doing so as to ensure that we are not being careless with our time and wasting our experience of life. No matter what task we undertake, we will do it wastefully if we assume that anything beyond the task itself will provide anything better than the experience of focus and presence in the task. There is nothing wrong with working toward and achieving wealth, fame, or power, but in the Stoic's mind, these things are merely to be enjoyed if they do work out, but not to be depended on for one's happiness. Because, if one is dependent on them, one's happiness and peace in life are especially susceptible to being inconsistent, taken, or never achieved at all.

Stoicism argues that the sign of a truly successful person is someone who can be ok without the things he or she typically desires or depends on for comfort. Wealth, materialistic abundance, fame, and power have no value in a happy life if the person who possesses them has not yet learned to live properly without them. Roman Emperor and Stoic philosopher Marcus Aurelius was, in his time, the most powerful person in the world. He had access to anything he ever wanted, yet he wrote, "Almost nothing material is needed for a happy life for he who has understood existence." With access to the world, Marcus Aurelius lived with little interest in the indulgence of things outside himself.

In order to develop this fortitude, a common practice in Stoicism is to, on occasion, temporarily strip oneself of the things one ordinarily depends on for comfort in order to prove how strong one truly is without them. In the piece of classic literature entitled *Letters from a Stoic*, the Roman statesman and renowned Stoic philosopher Seneca wrote, "Until we have begun to go without them, we fail to realize how unnecessary many things are. We've been using them not because we needed them but because we had them." It is perhaps in our constant expectation that something outside of ourselves or in the future is needed for a worthwhile experience in life that causes our inability to ever find worthwhile experience in life in the first place.

In *Letters from a Stoic*, Seneca also discusses the idea of how to properly handle one's time and derive meaningful experience from it. When referring to time, Seneca wrote:

> I advise you . . . to keep what is really yours; and you cannot begin too early. For, as our ancestors believed; it is too late to spare when you reach the dregs of the cask. Of that which remains at the bottom, the amount is slight, and the quality is vile.

It is now that we must find time and it is now that we must find happiness if it is either that we are seeking, because if we do not focus the lens through which we view life right now, everything we see from this moment forward will remain out of focus. For the Stoic, the ability to find happiness in spite of what occurs around us is developed through character and perspective. We must realize that nothing is good or bad inherently; only our judgments and interpretations of things can be good or bad. "The wise man,"

Seneca wrote, "is neither raised up by prosperity nor cast down by adversity; for always he has striven to rely predominantly on himself, and to derive all joy from himself." In other words, we must try to form our perspective to best serve our ability to remain with happiness and wonder regardless of the ups and downs of life.

Stoicism also claims that we are but a tiny feature of the entire body of nature, and everything that happens to us is a matter of relevance and necessity to everything beyond us. In this, we must strive for an acceptance and indifference to everything that happens, and instead, focus our attention on controlling our reactions to the things that happen. With this, we can begin to free ourselves from the chaos of the world and find some form of happiness and presence within ourselves.

The practice of Stoicism is not easy, and arguably, to live a completely Stoic life is impossible. Likely no person can be without moments of desire or negative reactions to the world around them. However, Stoicism gifts us with a target of wisdom to aim for—a happiness and calmness to strive for when things are at their apparent worst.

Starting from birth, we seemingly run, if not sprint, through life, racing out of every moment, unsatisfied with what life is and constantly looking to the future for what life could be if we could just obtain something more or different. Our cultures overwhelm us with the reinforcement of this idea, convincing us that our duty is to achieve, buy, own, and live perfect, unaffected lives. This delusion, however, frenzies us with an anxiety that we are then told, by culture, that we can rid ourselves of if we just achieve a few more things, make a little more money, be a little more popular, and buy a little more stuff, creating an endless feedback loop of unsatisfied hunger. If we cave into this, we surrender our life, we give up our self. In the words of Seneca, "We should not, like sheep, follow the herd of creatures in front of us, making our way where others go, not where we ought to go."

In the Stoic view, the things we often find ourselves chasing in life reveal themselves to be rather petty and meaningless from a sufficient distance. We don't have much, if any, control over what happens to us, how people see and treat us, or what happens because of what we do, and in the big picture, none of it really matters all that much anyway. And so, we must define our happiness not by what we own or achieve, not by how others see us, not by some bigger picture of life, but by how we think and see our self and live our own life through what we deem virtuous and relevant. Stoicism tells us we can at last, if we wish, calmly accept our indifferent reality and counter it with our own indifferent attitude in return.

WHY WE WORRY ALL THE TIME & HOW TO STOP

We seem to be some part of the punch line to a cruel joke. To consciously navigate this existence with the desire for safety, triumph, calmness, and certainty hardwired into us, all while being stricken by the specter of death, a fragile body, and a mysterious, fluctuating, indifferent universe. There are, have been, and will continue to forever be things to worry about as long as this dichotomy exists.

There is no shortage of reasons to worry. How absurd it would be to not, at least some of the time, feel worried about the absurdity of everything. But of course, after a point, worrying about the future, the unknown, and the potential for things to go wrong is nothing but a useless handicap.

We know that over-worrying can sometimes be just as much of a problem as not worrying at all. But this balance, like most balances, is complex. How much concern for the future is enough? And how much is not? And how does one find out and reconcile this balance without making the whole problem worse?

Stoicism is one philosophy in particular that focuses a good portion of its attention on addressing this problem of worrying. A key principle of Stoicism is understanding that if the only thing we can completely control in life is our internal domain, and we cannot truly control anything external, then one should try to maintain an awareness that the things we are concerned about could and very likely might happen, that life will contain moments of tragedy and sharp turns, and that we should be prepared for these moments both mentally and practically in any way we can. But equally important is recognizing that many of these sorts of catastrophic moments can't be predicted nor controlled, and thus, after a point, worrying is pointless. Once one has done everything that is rationally and realistically preventative, one should work to revert their attention back to the present, leaving all additional concern about the future for the future. Awareness and rational preparation have value in the future at low cost to the present. But worrying about what one cannot know nor control in the future has no value to either, and comes at the cost of the present.

Following the Stoic way of thinking, to potentially help counter this unnecessary anxiety and bring our attention and enjoyment back to the present, we can remind ourselves that in the future, things might not be ok, but if that is the case, then they must, by comparison, be ok now. And if we are worried that things will only get worse, then, if this comes true, things are as good as they'll ever be right now. And how foolish it would be to ruin what might be ok now out of concern for things potentially not being so later, especially if one cannot know nor do anything further to prevent it?

Moreover, we tend to assume the worst. We tend to worry not only about things going wrong, but the worst cases of things going wrong. However, how often does this actually turn out to be the case? Seneca wrote, "We are more often frightened than hurt; and we suffer more from imagination than from reality." Epictetus similarly wrote, "Man is not worried by real problems so much as by his imagined anxieties about real problems." In all likeliness, there is someone somewhere right now living some version of a seemingly worst-case scenario for many of us, living with no phone, computer, TV, and without a great many other things, unaware of a huge portion of the happenings of the world, and he or she is likely no less happy than many of us right now. We are adaptable creatures, wired to adjust our worries to our circumstances, as well as our ability to remain ok in the face of them. It is of great use to consider and meditate on this idea frequently and with confidence. Even if you end up facing the worst-case scenario, you would likely still be some form of ok. The ingredients of your being that have gotten you where you are, that have given you what you've experienced, will still remain. To paraphrase the Roman statesman and philosopher Cicero, *while one still breathes, one still has hope. At least, in some form.*

In no way is this to make light of the pain of enduring and recovering from hardships in life. There is a spectrum of human horrors, some far worse and more trying than others. In some cases, it is largely improbable to recover in the true sense of the term. But even if this is true, and one is worried about these sorts of horrible things happening, then again, they haven't happened yet.

In truth, how many things have we been worried about in the past that haven't crossed our minds since the moments we first worried about them? And what have we never worried about before that we are unfathomably worried about right now? How often has time erected or eroded our worries in new but equal form? How often has the world ended, but hasn't? How often has everything collapsed, but hasn't? How often has everything gone worst case, but hasn't? This does not mean that things have never collapsed, that they never turn out in the worst way, or even that the world could not end, but proportionally, it's rarely worth the bet. The French Renaissance philosopher and writer Michel de Montaigne wrote, "My life has been full of terrible misfortunes most of which never happened."

Many of us know all of this, at least in some form or another. In general, we likely have or could logically conclude that worrying about what hasn't happened or what we can't do anything about only adds or creates unnecessary suffering. But yet, most of us keep worrying. Like with most difficult things, there are paradoxes and ironies found in trying to implement these sorts of simple-seeming ideas. To try to resolve one's excessive worrying requires one being worried about one's worrying, at least to an extent. One can't use worry against worry to eliminate it. And so, realistically, despite Stoic ideas being so obvious and perhaps simple, in practice, we might always remain trapped in some amount of unnecessary worry, as this is inextricably linked with the human condition. As a consequence, perhaps our goal should be reducing unnecessary worry, rather than removing it entirely. Perhaps by accepting that one will always feel unease and that this is a natural part of the tragic backstory of human life, paradoxically, one might worry a little less about worrying as a whole. If we shouldn't stress over what we can't change or control outside of ourselves, perhaps at a point, we shouldn't stress about what we can't control inside of ourselves either.

Of course, all we can do is try our best, and try our best to not worry about whether or not our best resolves the impossible. Because, in truth, there is likely no heroic, ultimate defeat of worry, but only small, mini victories, moment to moment, along the way.

Human history is carved through trenches. We dip in and out of oscillating hardships, founded or unfounded. We are plagued by plagues and hatred and conflict and mortal fragility. But if we are fortunate enough to worry about something that is potentially not survivable happening to us as opposed to trying to survive something that already has, it is perhaps worth trying to be ok while we still are.

LIFE IS NOT SHORT, WE JUST WASTE MOST OF IT

The Philosophy of Seneca

It's not that we have a short time to live but that we waste most of it.

Lucius Annaeus Seneca

Lucius Annaeus Seneca, most commonly referred to as just Seneca, is recognized as one of the forefathers of Stoic philosophy. He was born around 4 BC in Spain but lived most of his life in Rome, until he died there in 65 AD. Throughout his life, he was a statesman, orator, writer of tragic plays, philosopher, and a variety of other things. He lived a life of rather extreme ups and downs as a result of his role in the politics of Rome. In a lot of ways, he can be observed to have struggled to follow what would be considered his own Stoic advice, which is perhaps worth noting. However, arguably, it does not devalue many of the ideas he shared, but rather, attests to their difficulty.

As mentioned, a leading Stoic principle is that we lack a great deal of control over the outcomes and happenings of our external world, and we can only ultimately choose, if anything, how we choose to perceive the unfolding of it. One particular condition that we are subjected to that Seneca focused much of his discourse on is time—in particular, how to handle our slippery and transient experience of it.

Seneca observed that we tend to be frugal and prudent with many aspects of our life. We tend to hoard our money and possessions and whatever else we can get our hands on, and yet, when it comes to time, we rarely guard it or evaluate carefully how well we save and spend it. He suggested that we often give up a great deal of our time to things and people that we wouldn't consider to be worthy of giving anything to if we slowed down and thought about what we were doing and why. "Men are thrifty in guarding their private property, but as soon as it comes to wasting time, they are most extravagant with the one commodity for which it's respectable to be greedy," wrote Seneca in his essay and letter entitled *On The Shortness of Life*.

Time, in Seneca's mind, is to be viewed like any other commodity—and if anything else, it is to be viewed as the most valuable one. Ultimately, all we have are our minds and our time. No one ever knows how much time they have inside their mind, and once it's gone, you can't work for, buy, or fight for it back. And yet, we seem to continue to treat our time like it's more or less infinite, and more or less inferior to the other objects in our possession.

Unlike the majority of possessions in life, you can't see, hold, or truly know time, making it incomprehensibly slippery and abstract. Seneca thought that because the present is so brief and immaterial, we mostly struggle to properly perceive and value it. For Seneca, to confront the concept of time, one must first fully confront the conditions of one's relationship with its finitude and accept one's fate as an observer or sort of passenger to it—that we are slipping in every moment toward the end of all moments, and, at any moment, it could all be cut short. And you can't do anything about it. This, although bleak, is worth often considering because the likely fact is that if everyone who was going to lose their life in the next couple of years knew they would, most of those people would live differently. And thus, we must live not as if we are one of the ones who will live into old age, but rather, one of the ones who might not. Only in such a case can the finitude of life begin to reveal itself. And only when the finitude of life reveals itself can we live in a way that might resemble how a finite life should be lived.

Of course, this is no small feat. The difference between imagining that life might end next week or in a couple of years is vastly different than knowing it will for a fact—and to know and manage this balance between now and later is perhaps one of the greatest challenges the human mind is faced with. But Seneca, like many other great philosophers, believed that we can and must work to overcome our tendency to look toward the future for solace, and rather, better focus our perspective on the present. This is essential, not only because the future might not come, but because even if it does, if we remain stuck in a constant preparatory cycle, when it arrives, it'll just be another moment to spend preparing and longing for further future moments. Seneca wrote:

> It is inevitable that life will be not just very short but very miserable for those who acquire by great toil what they must keep by greater toil. They achieve what they want laboriously; they possess what they have achieved anxiously; and meanwhile they take no account of time that will never more return. New preoccupations take the place of the old, hope excites more hope and ambition more ambition. They do not look for an end to their misery, but simply change the reason for it.

For Seneca, to hope to live for oneself finally in the future is to wait until it's too late. Rather, to make the most of time is to make the most of today. "Lay hold of today's task and you will not need to depend so much upon tomorrow's," he wrote.

Seneca believed that one should spend their time fulfilling their duties and responsibilities, enjoying any wealth and fortune that might come of them, but not work for the purpose of social status or material success beyond one's minimal needs, because beyond almost everything else, he argued for allocating as much time as possible to leisure—more specifically, a particular type of well-focused leisure in which one finds tranquility, introspection, and stillness. To be busily engaged in doing nothing is not valuable productivity, and to spend one's free time doing things that are of no real personal value is not well-used leisure. Both are but clever ways of wasting time. "The truly leisured person," Seneca wrote, "is one who is also conscious of his own leisure." The most valuable use of leisure, in his mind, is philosophy—time spent on intellectual reflections in which one recognizes, feels, and observes deeply the life that is being sifted through in each moment.

It seems that, in this, the worthiest use of time is in some sense spending it on reflecting on time itself. By considering, or at least pondering time and how to best use it, one is paradoxically using it well. Seneca described the value of this sort of reflection like that of securing the fluidity of time within the confines of a glass, containing it properly in order to see and possess it. The study of life and time helps us, in his mind, deepen the experience of the very life and time we are studying, allowing us to fill ourselves with wisdom, wonders, and connections from life's most potent access points. When referring to the study of intellectual maters, Seneca wrote:

> You really ought to leave ground level and turn your mind's eye to these studies ... In this mode of life much that is worth studying awaits you: the love and practice

of the virtues, forgetfulness of the passions, knowledge
of how to live and die, and deep repose.

Seneca believed wisdom to be timeless and thus the
primary thing worth pursuing and investing in—and
his words are around two thousand years old and yet
are still thought to have value.

In truth, it's fair to argue that no matter who you
are and what philosophy you believe in or follow, no
one truly knows how to fully wrestle with the concept
of time and win—or if philosophical contemplations
are the best use of one's time. Perhaps claiming to
know how anyone should spend their time is some
amount conceited. And to know why anyone should
do anything instead of nothing, or nothing instead of
anything, isn't self-evident. It perhaps, like most things,
comes down to the individual preference—a question
of what one deems valuable for themselves, and more
importantly, how well they act on what they deem
valuable for themselves. Wasted time or well-spent
time is all the same when viewed from a sufficient distance, and it is only the individual who can examine,
consider, and determine the best way to balance and
claim their time in each moment. And, of course, all
anyone can ever do is try their best.

There is clear value in now, and thus, there is clear
value in the *nows* yet to come—value that we must
consider when treating the now we are in, but not
to the extent that there is no value left in either. The
balancing act of now and later is nearly an impossi-

ble feat, but it is only in the examination of time that we get to consider such a problem. And it is perhaps only in the consideration of such a problem that we can feel the wonder that is the blender of human consciousness—a sense of confusion wrapped in intrigue, curiosity, and the desire to find resolution.

Ultimately, Seneca and his Stoic affiliates help provide a bridge to the realm of thought and wisdom. They help illuminate the forms of abstract things, like time, so we can better see them, create the fortitude to grapple with them, as well as develop a sense of consolation to help us be ok when we lose.

PART II

THE MEANING IN
THE NOTHINGNESS

Throughout my life, I have perhaps found the greatest solace and sense of meaning in the works of some of history's so-called darkest and most pessimistic thinkers. It might sound ironic for this to be the case—that meaning and comfort could be found in people and ideas that deny that life has any inherent meaning. But if you've ever been sad and put on sad music, you understand the value of dark, nihilistic, and pessimistic philosophy in the attempt to find light.

In a lot of ways, for me, philosophy is like music. It is often less about what it says and more about how it sounds and makes me feel. I don't come away from listening to a beautiful piece of music having learned anything concrete or academic about the world, but nonetheless, with the right song, I often feel I have learned all there is to know. To have learned nothing in concrete terms but feel as if I have learned everything in abstract terms is a profound and vital aesthetic experience. Philosophy, when presented in just the right way in just the right words at just the right time, has elicited this same sort of aesthetic experience. And the most intense aesthetic experiences, for me, come from tapping into the deeply poignant, honest places at the core of being—places that must come with sufficient darkness and sadness to be true.

What makes the sad song that I listen to when I'm in my worst of moods work is that it validates my feelings and transmutes them rather than denies them. I have found that this process of admitting and validating rather than denying is fundamental to the process of philosophy, meaning, and *truth*. The following essays cover ideas and philosophers that have helped me, and hopefully might help you, by pointing to the value in the difficulties and sufferings of life, not by denying them, but rather, by accepting and facing up to them.

FINDING MOTIVATION IN THE VOID

We have evolved through the ranks of our ancestors, outsmarting the other predators of the world, developing systems of material and nutritional exchange, creating health practices, and building incomprehensibly advanced technologies to facilitate longevity, safety, and efficiency. We have reached the top of this world, and yet, a great many of us see nothing from it.

As our awareness has progressed alongside everything else, we have found ourselves outgrowing more comfortable, shortsighted narratives of life and moving into a realm in which there appears to be no clear narrative or reason at all, but rather, an absurdity and meaninglessness underpinning everything. This is perhaps one of, if not the greatest contemporary issue of humankind—finding motivation and a sense of meaning in a period of time in which existence has revealed itself to be, or at least appears to be, meaningless.

Arguably, motivation to live and live meaningfully cannot be founded on the idea that life is a universally meaningful or ultimately resolvable thing if one finds that, at its core, it isn't. Motivation, rather, must go beneath the banal clichés of traditional ideals of happiness, success, and absolute meaning, and address the very real, bleak nature of our reality.

There is in fact no one-size-fits-all prescription or cheat-sheet or instruction manual to life, and there is likely no ultimate circumstance, idea, or thing that will make life's uncertainty, pain, and chaos go away. Realizing and accepting this is the first step. Only then can we consider what might actually be real and enduring.

In his novel, *Breakfast of Champions*, American author Kurt Vonnegut writes about an imaginary conversation between two yeast cells:

> They were discussing the possible purposes of life as they ate sugar and suffocated in their own excrement. Because of their limited intelligence, they never came close to guessing that they were making champagne.

In this little anecdote, Vonnegut alludes to the idea that with a limited intelligence, like our own, comes a limited ability to see the larger picture of which we are truly a part of. In this metaphor, the yeast cells are making champagne, something relatively insignificant, but rather nice nonetheless, which is perhaps a pleasant thought. However, by the same token, it could also be something not so nice. The point is that, like the yeast cells, we are, in essence, merely passengers in this thing, and we don't know what we are working toward or why or if it is even any good for us or about us at all. We could all be aggressively and competitively working toward something worse than this or indifferent to us. Or perhaps not. The only real and honest conclusion is that we don't know.

At first, this idea of not knowing what we are all doing might make things feel absurd and meaningless, and that's fair. However, the following step is to realize that this permits us to no longer be subservient to some specific grand meaning or template of life, that we don't have to discover or join in on someone else's ultimate answer or way of living, nor should we live in hopes of some future ideal or afterlife. Rather, we should attempt to follow our own barometers of meaning and believe in the only thing we have any evidence to believe in at all: ourselves and our relationship with this little sliver of time and space.

Some of the greatest minds in history have found that there appear to be layers or processes of the *self*. And if circumstances are sufficient and effort is directed toward understanding these layers, we move toward a truer or higher self—a self-realization of personal purpose and meaning. This idea was proposed by the psychologist Abraham Maslow in his hierarchy of needs, which is represented by a five-tier pyramid diagram that illustrates the order and balance of human needs, starting with material and physiological needs like food, water and safety, then moving into psychological needs like love and esteem, and then finally into self-actualization, or living according to one's true self and one's full potential. Somewhat similarly, this idea of a truer, maximized self was also alluded to by the renowned psychologist Carl Jung in his concept of *individuation*, which suggests that there is a ring of layers that comprises our self: our outward, social personas, our conscious layers, our unconscious layers, and then a core, true self at the center of it all, which when one goes through the process of uncovering and integrating every layer into consciousness, a sense of completeness, harmony, and vitality is experienced in the form of a truer self. These concepts, along with others unmentioned, suggest that we each have a sort of core self that provides a source of meaning unique to us—a source that points us to the things that we actually want and should do with our life. The things we are motivated by, therefore, must not be merely to impress others nor achieve anything according to any societal ideals, because everyone has their own unique, complicated source of motivation that leads to distinctive outputs. There are certainly shared common ideas and ways to approach life that are worth considering, but one must attempt to consider how each of them fit with one's own self before assuming them.

The mass of despairing individuals are not disillusioned because life is inherently meaningless, but because they willingly let themselves be pulled from their own individual meaning, distracted and tempted by the idea that somehow, through enough surplus money and possessions and achievements of this and that according to other people's ideas and constructions, life could be made completely happy and perfect and certain. However, no matter what one does, no one can do this. What one can seem to do, however, is follow, discover, and create a personal meaningfulness that endures the fact that life can never be completely happy, perfect, or certain.

The acceptance and realization of one's *self* and the creation of personal meaning is unfathomably difficult to process and understand, let alone do. It is perhaps the true challenge of human existence. However, it is a worthy and possible one—an arduous process one must work on and fight for until the lights go out.

We are perhaps the only stop on this evolutionary train that is outside the tunnel of darkness, able to take the material of everything and make it into something beautiful or helpful or interesting, to understand and create the meaning of meaning itself. And to do so just because we can, because the universe, for some reason, gave us a blank page to write on.

FACE THE PAIN
OF LIFE

The Philosophy of
Arthur Schopenhauer

Being one of the first philosophers to ever really question the value of existence, to systematically combine Eastern and Western modes of thinking, and to introduce the arts as a serious philosophical focus, Arthur Schopenhauer is perhaps one of the most comprehensive philosophers in Western history—and also one of the darkest.

Schopenhauer was born in 1788 in what is now Gdansk, Poland, but spent the majority of his childhood in Hamburg, Germany, after his family moved there when he was five. He was born into a wealthy family, his father being a highly successful international merchant. Throughout early life, young Schopenhauer was expected to follow in his father's footsteps. However, from an early age, he had no interest in business, and instead, found himself drawn to academics. On a trip around Europe with his parents to prepare him for his merchant career, the greater exposure he would receive to the pervasive suffering and poverty of the world would cause him to become all the more interested in pursuing this path of scholarship and intellectual examination of how the world worked and why—or perhaps more accurately, how and why it appeared to work so negatively.

After eventually turning away from his family's readymade path of international business, Schopenhauer would attend the University of Göttingen in 1809, where, in his third semester, he would become further focused on philosophy. The following year, he would transfer to the University of Berlin, but Schopenhauer would soon find academic philosophy to be unnecessarily obscure, detached from the real concerns of life, and often tethered to theological agendas, all of which he despised. Eventually, he left the academic, intellectual circuit and spent the following decade philosophizing and writing on his own.

By age thirty, Schopenhauer had published the two works that would go on to define his entire career and contain the complete unified philosophical system from which he would never deviate and that would eventually influence the entire course of Western thinking. The foundation of his philosophy was established in his dissertation, *On the Fourfold Root of the Principle of Sufficient Reason*, published in 1813. His entire unified philosophical system, including his metaphysics, epistemology, ethics, aesthetics, value judgments, and so forth, was then later laid out in his subsequent mas-terwork, *The World as Will and Representation*, published in 1819. Despite these impressive works going on to occupy a central role in Western philosophy and influencing some of the greatest subsequent thinkers and schools of thought, during his life, they would go mostly unnoticed.

Over the decades following his early work, through-out his thirties and forties, Schopenhauer would spend his time working as a lecturer at university as well as a translator of French-to-English prose, while continuing to write on and off on the side. He found very little success in any of it. Only in his fifties did Schopenhauer finally start to receive any recognition, and only after publishing a book of essays and apho-risms in 1851 would he achieve fame. In 1860, he died at the age of seventy-two.

In terms of the philosophical system established within Schopenhauer's work, it is relevant to note that it leaned heavily on the work of his predecessor, Immanuel Kant. In Schopenhauer's mind, he was completing Kant's system of *transcendental idealism*. Building on his interpretation of Kant, Schopenhauer essentially suggested that the world as we know and experience it is exclusively a representation created by our mind through our senses and forms of cogni-tion. Consequently, we cannot access the true nature of external objects outside our mental, phenomeno-logical experience of them. Deviating from Kant, Schopenhauer would go on to argue that not only can we not know nor access the varying objects of the world as they really are outside of our conscious experience, but there is, in fact, no plurality of objects beyond our experience at all. Rather, beyond our experience is, according to Schopenhauer, a singular, unified oneness of reality—a sort of essence or force that drives existence that is beyond time, beyond space, and beyond all objectivation. Schopenhauer would go on to explore and define this force by referencing and probing into the experience of living within the body, suggesting that this is the only thing in the world that we have access to that is not solely a mental representation of an object but is also a firsthand, subjective experience from within it. From here, Schopenhauer would suggest that what is found from within, at the core of our being, is an unconscious, restless force striving toward survival, nourishment, and reproduction. He would term this force the *Will*. Essentially, this would lead him to the conclusion that reality is made up of two sides: the plurality of things as they are represented to a conscious apparatus, and the singular, unified force of the Will—hence the name of his masterwork, *The World as Will and Representation*.

It is worth noting that the term *Will* can perhaps be misleading in that it might seem to imply an intention or human-like conscious motivation, but the Will, for Schopenhauer, is a blind, unconscious striving with no goal or purpose other than to keep itself going for the sake of keeping itself going. All of the material world operates by and through this Will, moving, striving, consuming, and violently expressing itself in order to sustain itself.

Schopenhauer's work was largely a response to Kant and the Western philosophical tradition, but his work also contains distinct notes of Hinduism and Buddhism. His conclusion about the nature of reality is strikingly similar to that of both religions, and his assessment of reality's negative relationship with the conscious self mirrors ideas central to Buddhism. This made Schopenhauer one of the first philosophers to ever really combine Eastern and Western thinking in a systematic and comprehensive way.

In a way that is especially similar to Buddhism, Schopenhauer would top off his philosophical medley with a layer of dark, unwavering pessimism:

> Unless suffering is the direct and immediate object of life, our existence must entirely fail of its aim. It is absurd to look upon the enormous amount of pain that abounds everywhere in the world, and originates in needs and necessities inseparable from life itself, as serving no purpose at all and the result of mere chance. Each separate misfortune, as it comes, seems, no doubt, to be something exceptional; but misfortune in general is the rule.

As an assessment of the nature of reality, he would describe the Will as a sort of malevolent force that we, as individual selves, become victims of in its process of continuation, deceived by our own mind and body to go against our fundamental interests and yearnings in order to carry it out. Since the Will has no aim or purpose other than its perpetual continuation, then the Will can never be satisfied. And since we are expressions of it, neither can we. Thus, we are driven to consume beings, things, ideas, goals, circumstances, and all the rest, constantly hoping that we will feel satisfaction or happiness as a result, while constantly being left in the wake of each achievement unsatisfied. Schopenhauer wrote:

> Human life must be some kind of mistake. The truth of this will be sufficiently obvious if we only remember that man is a compound of needs and necessities hard to satisfy; and that even when they are satisfied, all he obtains is a state of painlessness, where nothing remains to him but abandonment to boredom.

As the best possible ways of sort of escaping and dealing with this, Schopenhauer would put forth two primary methods: one, engaging in arts and philosophy, and two, the practice of asceticism: the deprivation of nearly all desire, self-indulgence, and material comfort. In this latter method, Schopenhauer felt that by denying the Will from being fed, so to speak, one would turn the Will against itself and overcome it. However, he also recognized the sheer difficulty of this for the majority of people and suggested that the average person should simply make their best efforts to let go of ideals of happiness and pleasure, and instead, focus on the minimization of pain. Happiness in life, for Schopenhauer, is not a matter of joys and pleasures, but rather, the reduction of and freedom from pain as much as possible. "The safest way of not being very miserable is not to expect to be very happy," he wrote.

Alternatively, engaging in arts and philosophy, in Schopenhauer's mind, served as another, more accessible method. He felt that 'good' art could provide a source of clarity into the nature and problems of being, without any of the illusion or false decoration. And while engaging in this sort of art, one would have a transcendent-like experience that provides relief and comfort from the pain of existence. With this concept, Schopenhauer would be one of first thinkers to ever really ascribe philosophical significance to the arts, and he would eventually become known by many as the *artist's philosopher*.

Throughout his work in general, Schopenhauer makes large, often unprovable claims about the nature of reality and the value of existing within it, some of which are validly constructed and worth considering, but some of which are not. Ultimately, any attempt to define and assess the part of reality beyond logic through logic itself is perhaps paradoxical in a way that is beyond repair. What precisely is the Will, where does it come from, where does it end, and how can we know or prove it? And in terms of Schopenhauer's suggestion that one should turn against the Will through an ascetic process of self-denial, if all of life operates through the Will, to turn against it would seem to merely be the Will turning against the Will for reasons that favor it. There can be no turning against the Will if the Will is doing the turning.

Alternatively, considering the view of Friedrich Nietzsche, a philosopher who notably followed in Schopenhauer's footsteps, the endless cycle of desire and dissatisfaction caused by the Will is actually a good thing that we can use as fuel toward the process of self-overcoming and growth, from which we can then distill life's meaning. Of course, this is the more pleasant of the two interpretations, but it isn't clear which is apt or accurate, if either.

Ultimately, Schopenhauer is another surprising, yet seemingly common story of a highly important thinker, artist, or writer who barely caught any recognition in their lifetime, only to die and end up with their name in history books. One trait these stories do all seem to have in common, though, is a refusal to stop, a refusal to budge from pursuing and defending a vision of the world as one sees it. Schopenhauer never deviated from the philosophical system he created in his twenties and never stopped confidently working to build upon it and reinforce it throughout his life, despite the world seeming to suggest to him that he should do otherwise. And now, it is hugely significant to the world that he did exactly what he did. For some, his work might be bleak and disconcerting, but for others, his work, like all great works of dark, melancholic honesty, is comforting, relieving, and legitimizing. It reminds us that we are not crazy, and that our sadness and suffering are not unfounded, even when it feels that way. We are merely born into a crazy, sad, violent reality with a mind and body that are often all in conspiracy against us. Because of this, and many other reasons unmentioned, Schopenhauer's work has influenced artists like Richard Wagner and Gustav Mahler, writers like Marcel Proust, Leo Tolstoy, and Samuel Beckett, and thinkers like Friedrich Nietzsche, Sigmund Freud, and Ludwig Wittgenstein, ultimately influencing the course of modern thinking.

Having been one of the first to properly and philosophically bring the value of life and the possibility of meaning into question, Schopenhauer helped locate the budding problem of the growing agnostic world that philosophy would need to address. With humanity seemingly suspending further out into a void of meaning, his unyielding and fearless confrontation with the nature of existence, including all its horrors and miseries, revealed the possibility of finding new answers from within.

BECOME WHO YOU REALLY ARE

The Philosophy of Friedrich Nietzsche

Positioned at the forefront of perhaps the most significant shift in Western history, having predicted both its causes and consequences, and going on to provide grandiose, revolutionary ideas as possible solutions, Friedrich Nietzsche is one of the most influential and significant thinkers in modern history.

The crossroads that Nietzsche stood at was one where the primary path of Western religious faith began to crumble and cave in, leaving a massive, empty crater at the end of life's suffering with what seemed like only one alternative path: one that led toward pessimism and nihilism. His life's work would take on this newly emerging issue and attempt to forge a new, third path away from both religious faith and nihilism, and toward new meaning and human values.

Nietzsche was born in 1844 in Saxony, Prussia, which is now part of eastern Germany. He was born to a modest family, living an ordinary, sheltered childhood. His father, Carl Ludwig Nietzsche, was the town's Lutheran pastor, which would immediately immerse young Nietzsche into Christianity. However, simultaneous to being introduced to it, his faith would soon be challenged and tested, as his father, the same man who practiced and preached of God, was diagnosed with a terminal brain disease. For a year, Nietzsche's father suffered horribly and then died at the age of just thirty-five. The following year, Nietzsche's younger brother, Ludwig, also died. This dichotomy of his religious foundation and early exposure to the irreconcilable, reasonless pain and suffering experienced by good, underserving people, would likely lay some of the foundation for what would ultimately become the basis of Nietzsche's later work.

Following a fairly somber, serious, and lonely childhood, Nietzsche would go on to study theology at the University of Bonn. Both in early schooling and at university, he would show strong intellectual promise, excelling especially in Christian theology. However, following just one semester at university, as he became increasingly critical and sharp, and after he was exposed to various critiques of Christianity, Nietzsche would have no choice but to let go of his Christian faith, fully shedding the skin of his innocence and blind devotion. He would then go on to study philology, the study of the history of language, at the

University of Leipzig. Here, he would do so well that while still only in his mid-twenties, he would be hired as a professor of classical philology at the University of Basel, becoming the youngest professor to ever be hired, still to this day.

After only a few years of teaching, Nietzsche would leave his position, partly because of his growing dissatisfaction and sense of constraint within academia, and partly because of his increasingly poor health: a combination of genetic ailments and what is believed to have been a case of syphilis that he contracted at a brothel. From here, he would go on to live a fairly isolated life, traveling around Europe, moving to and from different climates that were suitable for his poor health, and living off his small university pension. He would live primarily and most notably in the Swiss Alps, where he would spend the majority of his remaining sane life.

Throughout this time, in between spells of being bed ridden by his ailments, a devastating failed love ordeal, degrading friendships and family relations, and depressive and nihilistic states, Nietzsche would spend most of his time walking, thinking, and writing, finding solace, meaning, and reason to continue through his pursuit of philosophy. Out of this, he would produce many influential works, including *Human All Too Human*, *The Gay Science*, *Thus Spoke Zarathustra*, *Beyond Good and Evil*, and *On the Genealogy of Morals*. In these works, Nietzsche would lay the groundwork and sketch out the floor plan for a new sort of philosophy—a philosophy that would essentially loosen the bolts of all contemporary certainties, all notions of good and evil, all knowledge of true and false, right and wrong. In *The Gay Science* Nietzsche wrote:

> God is dead. God remains dead. And we have killed him. How shall we comfort ourselves, the murderers of all murderers? What was holiest and mightiest of all that the world has yet owned has bled to death under our knives . . . Is not the greatness of this deed too great for us? Must we ourselves not become gods simply to appear worthy of it?

This is perhaps one of Nietzsche's most quoted and important passages. It is in this line, "God is dead," that we find, not Nietzsche's celebration of humanity's lost faith, but his stark, intense concern for what it meant. The collapse of Christian faith brought with it, in Nietzsche's mind, the collapse of everything built on it—the whole of European morality, its rationales, and its values. He both predicted and feared that with this collective revelation, without sufficient replacement, humanity would be left to struggle with no clear system or meaning, and it would devolve into widespread despair in the form of nihilism.

One of Nietzsche's key ideas at the foundation of his attempt to resolve this issue is the recognition that there is in fact no universal, objective truth to be known. "There are no facts, only interpretations," he wrote. Nietzsche denied the very construct of any sort of truth with a capital T, and suggested that all attempts to find one were woefully misguided and actually the source of disconnection preventing modern man from rediscovering any meaning in life. The pursuit of universal objectivity or meaning in the world beyond this one took the spirit out of the present, earthly human experience of meaning, which is inherently subjective, independent, and expressive. Because of this, Nietzsche would direct his attention primarily to the arts and humanities, believing that creative acts and experiences like music, philosophy, literature, theater, and so on could be used as essential means to communicate deeper truths and fill the void of higher connection and meaning. Although, as Nietzsche explored this theory, he would find that the arts and humanities were susceptible to becoming dried out, academic, and commodified, often losing their luster and dependability. From here, he would turn his attention toward creating a philosophy that detached the individual from dependence on any collective experience or cultural mechanisms, and rather, focused on the individual pursuit of creative expression and subjective greatness, placing the creation of meaning squarely in the hands of the individual.

This philosophy would be embodied in what Nietzsche would term the *Übermensch*, or *overman*, which he would first introduce in his book *Thus Spoke Zarathustra*. The overman is described as a sort of defiant, confident, independent individual who pursues their personal desires with vigor and dignifies their independent beliefs unapologetically; someone who deviates from the collective, exhibits strategic self-ishness, and acts with aggressiveness and grandios-ity. The reason for such characteristics was justified, in Nietzsche's view, by the fact that a new morality that opposed the moral views rooted in Christianity, which praised weakness and modesty, was needed to better suit the natural condition of human experience, which he believed involved the desire for vigor, power, and greatness. This view is not without reasonable cri-tiques and unreasonable misinterpretations. However, perhaps what is more important than Nietzsche's image of the overman is what the concept serves to represent. In slightly broader terms, Nietzsche sets up the overman to function as a sort of idealized version of oneself—an image of a perfect and powerful being who has overcome all their fears and deficiencies, which one can and should set goals to strive toward. Of course, as an ideal, it cannot ever truly be reached, but that is functionally the point.

Nietzsche proposed that the world, including the human world, operates from a principle that he called *the will to power*: an insatiable desire in each liv-ing being to manifest power. "The world is the will to power—and nothing besides," he wrote. And accord-ing to Nietzsche, this will to power is manifested in the desire for personal growth and satisfied in the pursuit of said growth. It is important to note here that his notion of power does not necessarily refer to physical strength nor power and dominance over others, but rather, power over oneself. Psychological and spiritual strength in the form of self-mastery and continuous growth represents the ultimate synchronization with the will to power for Nietzsche, and thus, the ultimate synchronization with life itself. The desire and striving toward the ideal of the overman serves as perpetual fuel for this process of self-growth as one works through a continuous cycle of self-dissatisfaction, self-improvement, and self-rediscovery, over and over. For Nietzsche, this process, which he would term *self-overcoming*, is fundamental to answering and resolving the problem of meaning and value in life. So long as one establishes one's goals of growth in the name of what one deems to be an idealized, life-affirming version of themselves, the process transmutes the suffering of life into something worthwhile and personally redeemable—a sort of alchemy of the spirit that affirms life in the face of its inevitable suffering. "If we have our own why in life, we shall get along with almost any how," Nietzsche wrote.

Unlike his primary predecessor, Arthur Schopenhauer, who proposed that suffering is best minimized and avoided to the best of one's ability, Nietzsche argued that suffering is a good thing that should be leaned into, embraced, and used as fuel toward the amassing of strength and psychological power. Life is in fact inevitable suffering, and so, it is not a matter of *if*, but *for what?* "The meaninglessness of suffering, not suffering itself, was the curse that lay over mankind so far," Nietzsche wrote.

While continuing to write and live an increasingly isolated life in the mountains, still in the early stages of some of his most ambitious philosophical undertakings, Nietzsche would begin to show signs of declining mental health. At forty-four years old, after seeing a horse being flogged in a street by its owner, he experienced a mental breakdown, rushing over to the horse, hugging and consoling it, and yelling, "I understand you, I understand you!" This strange episode, which marked his last moments out of apparent lucidity, appeared to be an act of contradiction to his own philosophy: pity, weakness, and compassion. Soon after, Nietzsche would dip into complete madness, eventually falling into a state of catatonia. One of the most powerful minds of modern history seemingly collapsed under the weight of itself. Whether the cause was organic, the latent consequence of his contracted ailments, or the consequence of a mind that journeyed too far into itself and got stuck on its way back out, is unknown. Before ever coming back out, in 1900, Nietzsche died of a stroke at the age of fifty-five.

During his lifetime, according to his own standards, Nietzsche might have been considered a failure. Prior to losing his sanity, he had made very little of himself and saw very little success. His books didn't sell, and he never really garnered any respect or recognition. But following his death, of course, his work would take off, soon gaining massive attention, respect, and a worldwide following—some of which, unfortunately, would lead to horrible, misguided, and ill-conceived applications. However, today, and more generally, Nietzsche's work remains potent, important, and notably engrained in modern thinking. His quotes, aphorisms, and ideas echo through culture every day, both explicitly and implicitly. And so, in a fittingly ironic way, given that Nietzsche suggested that we must symbolically die throughout life so that we can get out of our own way and become something greater, sometimes sacrificing our self, our personal preservation, health, or sanity, perhaps Nietzsche's life and death was just that: a process of self-overcoming toward self-sacrifice toward something greater.

Of course, Nietzsche's ideas aren't without critiques, including the notions of self-overcoming, sacrifice, and greatness. Although his assessments and predictions of modern issues are quite accurate, his resolutions aren't necessarily successful for everyone. Is suffering in the continual pursuit of desire and self-destruction in the name of growth toward an unattainable end goal really a good thing? And how can one see it as a good thing if they do not? How can one create a life-affirming interpretation of life if their interpretation of life is not affirming? In other words, if someone sees life as negative or meaningless, how can they create goals that have any purpose? This person is stuck at square one, in need of some truth or meaning beyond themselves, something other than what they see, have, or experience, which they do not have. Furthermore, if one does not agree with the initial premise that suffering in the name of progress is good, then the rest might merely be misdirection.

Of course, being a philosopher whose work doesn't necessarily follow any linear or systematic structure, and which can even contradict itself at times, Nietzsche's ideas are open to multiple interpretations—and of course, all of the above is merely a single, very brief one. More importantly, seeing as how his philosophy caters to this open-ended nature, and is arguably not a guide to think in a certain way, but rather, a guide to think in one's own way, Nietzsche leaves us the space to, even if we disagree with him, do just as he did and pave a new path for ourselves.

DEALING WITH REGRETS (& WHAT YOU MIGHT REGRET)

Nietzsche on Amor Fati

If right now you were told that you would relive this life exactly how it has gone and exactly how it will go, with all its ups and downs, fortunes and tragedies, pleasures and pains, over and over for eternity, what would you think? Would you be terrified? Would you want to change it? Would you be happy with it? What could you do or think to make it ok, and perhaps even desirable?

Nietzsche used a version of this contemplation as a sort of thought experiment, referred to as the *eternal recurrence*, to help illustrate and consider one of his most notable philosophical tenets, known as *amor fati*. The phrase amor fati is Latin for *love of one's fate*. This concept is recognized to have first been referenced and discussed in the philosophical work of the Stoic philosophers Epictetus and Marcus Aurelius.

However, Nietzsche would be the first to explicitly use and focus on the phrase, molding and integrating it as a unique, important value in his philosophy. He would most notably discuss the idea in his books *The Gay Science*, *Ecce Homo*, as well as throughout other works, notes, and letters. Around the time Nietzsche was writing these works, he had retreated to the Swiss Alps and was experiencing what one could easily infer to be a period of deep self-reflection over a life that was spiked with hardships and failures. He had fled from his family and career in academia to find independence and pursue freelance writing. However, he could not escape the reverberating negative effects of his family, nor could he find success in his writing. He lost friendships, romances, and soon his mind. His health waned throughout middle age, and he would frequently be bed-ridden and in pain. His work was essentially all he had, and it was not enough—at least at the time. His books did not sell well, and his philosophy went mostly unnoticed. His life was beset with failure after failure, misery after misery, until he died a relatively horrible death. Of course, we now know that following Nietzsche's death, he would go on to become one of the most significant philosophical figures to ever live. And so, how did such a brilliant, philosophical mind deal with such a failure-ridden, dreadful existence? He attempted to philosophize it. He attempted to derive wisdom and understanding from it; he conceptualized and integrated his view of amor fati.

For Nietzsche, when referring to amor fati, he is arguably talking generally about the loving of one's life. Understanding the nuance in Nietzsche's use of the term love is important—it suggests more than a stoic acceptance, and instead, it connotes an almost enthusiastic and total adoration. It is a sentiment against the tendency to regret, to assume one could have retained more control over the outcomes and conditions of one's reality, to have done differently, to have known any better, to have found that an existence void of particular negatives would have ultimately netted more positives. And instead, it is a declaration of love and embrace of all of life exactly how it is, with all the good and the bad, the success and the failure, the satisfaction and the pain. Nietzsche described it in this way:

> My formula for greatness in a human being is amor fati: that one wants nothing to be different, not forward, not backward, not in all eternity. Not merely bear what is necessary, still less conceal it . . . but love it.

Naturally and understandably, we tend to find ourselves doing the opposite, deluded by the mirage of hindsight and wishful thinking. It appears as if there were options to have done differently, for things to have gone differently, to have been better. We regret what happens and yearn for otherness. In a theoretical sense, this may be true; there were potential different options to choose from in the past and different potential ways for things to go in the future. But in this reality, the one we must live, there was no option to have done differently, and there is no other way for things to go. Every decision you've made was the best and only decision you could've made at the time with the information you had and the state of mind you were in. And every condition of life that either these decisions led to or that are fundamental to life in general, you have no control over and cannot change.

To regret or desire to go back and edit the past assumes that the things we wish to change, presumably things we perceive and interpret as negative, are purely negative in the bigger picture—or that equally negative things would not have occurred if everything went differently. It assumes that one could know what is truly and ultimately best, how things would have gone if they went differently, and that somehow one would not still find oneself in a similar state of regret and loathing if they did.

It is not necessarily that life could have been different that is the problem, but that we resist finding the beauty in how it inevitably has gone. Resenting or fighting against what has happened to you or because of you only brings additional misery into the *now*, exasperating the problem and creating more to resent and resist. Like pouring the gasoline of regret onto a fire of unchangeable circumstances, we only unnecessarily intensify the flames.

The true challenge and task of life, for Nietzsche, is to fall in love with what you are actually experiencing right now, as it is, in all the ways it is. He wrote:

I want to learn more and more to see as beautiful what is necessary in things; then I shall be one of those who make things beautiful. Amor fati: let that be my love henceforth! I do not want to wage war against what is ugly. I do not want to accuse; I do not even want to accuse those who accuse. Looking away shall be my only negation. And all in all and on the whole: some day I wish to be only a Yes-sayer.

This overcoming of regret and loathing and resistance, the question posed in Nietzsche's eternal recurrence of whether or not you would want to live your life over, whether or not you love or could love your life, is not at all obvious or easy. In the previous quote, it should be noted that it concludes with the words, "some day I wish to be." Arguably, Nietzsche alluded to it as a challenge of existence because of how difficult and perhaps unlikely it is for most people to say *yes* to life in this way. Perhaps the notion of amor fati is more of an ideal that Nietzsche establishes to strive toward. Ultimately, to experience the moments of treachery and loneliness, failure and disaster, loss and death, and all the tragedies that pervade existence, and to still say *yes, I love it*, is perhaps impossible in a specific case-by-case sense. But perhaps in certain moments of high enough spirits, sufficiently distanced from misfortune, it is possible to practice a certain love for the whole of it. And for Nietzsche, achieving this is the greatest affirmation of life, which can then be used to construct the lens through which we see the beauty in everything and more frequently arrive at that resounding *yes*.

Ultimately, the question may not be how much you love your life right now, but how much you could and how. And perhaps sometimes the only way to experience the beauty of things is to think about things in a beautiful way.

Throughout his career, Nietzsche wrote extensively about the value of self-overcoming, achievement, vitality, and power—the constant defining and accomplishment of new goals set forth in the image of what one views as their ideal self—and yet, interestingly, and at first pass, counterintuitively, amor fati offers a much gentler and more passive sentiment. However, amor fati need not deny the notion of trying to overcome and accomplish, of trying to thrash and swim against the current of existence and achieve things within it or control where it takes us. Rather, one's fate includes this. It includes trying to overcome life's conditions and failing in some ultimate sense. And arguably, this idea of amor fati was, in its own right, a way of overcoming used by Nietzsche, and one that's available to those who adopt it—a way of overcoming this ultimate conclusion of self-overcoming: the unattainable ideal self and ideal life.

Amor fati is a sentiment of willingness to accept at last the way things have gone and will go, to love a life that tries in almost every moment to make you hate it, and to still stare back at it and say *yes, I love it.* What's scarier than an opponent who smiles while being beaten?

EMBRACE THE MEANINGLESSNESS

The Philosophy of Emil Cioran

Emil Cioran was a writer and philosopher born in 1911 in what is present day Rasinari, Romania. He is renowned for his penetratingly dark, nihilistic, yet beautiful writing style, considered by many to be one of the great writers of despair. His philosophical arguments are uniquely built off the somber, emotional rhythm of his prose, often expressing shocking thoughts and dark humor, nearly every sentence and passage hung down from the very heights of despair.

Born into a socially and spiritually volatile time in Western history, somewhere in the middle of the increasing disintegration of religious ideology and the newly emerging philosophical movements of idealism, pessimism, nihilism, and existentialism, Cioran would find himself positioned on the face of a mountain that humanity was desperately trying to get over. And from his view, he saw nothing—

a deathly climb to another valley of nowhere.

At a fairly young age, Cioran would become a heavy reader, going on to study literature and philosophy at the University of Bucharest, a public university in Romania. Here, he would read the works of philosophers like Immanuel Kant, Arthur Schopenhauer, Friedrich Nietzsche, Lev Shestov, Georg Hegel, and many others. At twenty-three, Cioran would publish his first book, titled *On the Heights of Despair*, which would soon go on to both receive critical acclaim and stir controversy, achieving him two notable awards and setting him on the path to becoming an internationally recognized writer and thinker.

In this first work, not only did Cioran reveal his promising, young intellectual mind, but also what would go on to become the reoccurring, lifelong themes and obsessions found in his other work— themes like despair, suffering, social isolation, absurdity, futility, failure, decay, and death. Written out of a spell of horrible insomnia, his first book would provide a foretelling of what awaited Cioran: a lifelong exploration of the underbelly of the human condition fueled by a depression-infused insomniac lifestyle. Cioran described it in this way:

> I've never been able to write otherwise than in the midst of the depression brought about by my nights of insomnia. For seven years I could barely sleep. I need this depression, and even today before I sit down to write I play a disk of Gypsy music from Hungary.

Like many great writers and artists, Cioran felt as though he had to write. It was not that he made his work sad, but that his sadness made his work. In the moments of depression, writing was, according to him, his only therapy. His first book, and the twenty plus others of his that were to come, according to Cioran, saved him from what might have otherwise seemed like the logical conclusion of much of his work. If nothing else, this aspect of his work and life reveals a profound insight into the potency of the creative process. Even in writing about the futility and meaninglessness of life and its endeavors, the power of the creative process can, in some sense, save the writer from the very content of their own work, paradoxically making the futility and meaninglessness of life that they discuss somewhat less futile and meaningless.

After leaving Romania in 1940, Cioran would end up living the majority of his life in Paris. He would go on to produce books written in both Romanian and French, maintaining the same eloquence, wit, and intensity throughout all of them. His work would increasingly develop and maintain his reputation amongst the most prominent of France's intellectuals, garnering the admiration of high-ranking philosophical peers as well as a large following of readers across the world. Despite this, he would live a very modest, private life, going to great lengths to avoid all accolades and any way of life that would otherwise be considered successful. In 1995, at the age of eighty-four, Cioran died after having developed Alzheimer's several years earlier. Slowly but surely, one of the most eloquent minds of the twentieth century lost all relationship with words and then experienced one of the main themes of his life's work firsthand: nothingness.

In terms of Cioran's philosophy, despite his work being unmistakably perceptive and intelligent, he is somewhat unique and perhaps debatable in the context of a *philosopher*. For the most part, traditional philosophical work is almost always grounded in a particular system of thought, which is formed or integrated first as a foundation and then logically built upon. Cioran's work, however, does not really start from nor integrate any real system of this kind. Rather, it relies more on his aphoristic, observational writing style, which seems to almost philosophize and reveal metaphysical ideas through the emotionally tense, subjective, and chaotic reading experience alone, without much consideration of logical structure or systematic reasoning. Seeing as how a key part of Cioran's philosophy was that he disagreed with the ability of traditional philosophy to use reason to resolve life and explain life's lack of reason, this approach makes sense. To adequately argue for a philosophy of absurdity and futility, what better way is there than to write without priority for structure or reason? In this sense, perhaps it would be more accurate to say that Cioran was sort of an *antiphilosophy* philosopher. Perhaps, ironically, this is still a philosophy.

According to what can be surmised of Cioran's views, it is more or less death specifically that both causes the futility of life as well as poses the inevitable limit to all reason within it. However, in his most famous work, *The Trouble with Being Born,* he discusses how since death necessarily follows from birth, it is actually the memory of our birth that is the tragic problem of life, and not death in and of itself. The attempt to reason an understanding of or solution to the conscious awareness of death stemming from birth is thus both the driving force of philosophy, religion, and science, and simultaneously the force that destroys them—the unbeatable opponent under which all reason, logic, and human effort crumble. Consequently, any philosophical attempt toward an understanding or solution, for Cioran, can only be a contemplation on failure. Broadly speaking, this concept would also become a fundamental tenet of his philosophy, Cioran often underpinning his ideas with the notion that human endeavors are almost always synonymous with failure.

What his work also seemed to parallel alongside this dread and nihilism, though, is the notion of accepting and playing into the absurdity of it all. It encourages us to love the absurd uselessness for what it is, how it is, and to use it against itself and live anyway. In the words of Cioran:

When all the current reasons—moral, esthetic, religious, social, and so on—no longer guide one's life, how can one sustain life without succumbing to nothingness? Only by a connection with the absurd, by love of absolute uselessness, loving something which does not have substance but which simulates an illusion of life. *I live because the mountains do not laugh and the worms do not sing.*

It is in this dive into the absurdity that Cioran seems to pose the following question: can those who accept and embrace failure and disaster ever really fail or be struck by either? Pessimism, in this sense, almost serves as a trump card—the last true failure being the failure of optimism. From there, we become, as he put it, "invincible victims."

There is a certain unique and important quality to the irony of Cioran's work. As a sort of *antiphilosophy* philosopher who argued that life cannot be reconciled into something meaningful, he nonetheless did so by philosophizing (at least in some form). The philosophy of nihilism, with which he is generally associated, denies the value of all things. But can a nihilist philosophy be expressed as a philosophy and remain a nihilist philosophy? In other words, can the premise and conclusion be that life is inherently meaningless and that endeavoring and seeking reason is entirely futile, while simultaneously making this meaningful claim through creative action and, albeit subversively, providing reasons for it? Discussing or creatively expressing the notion that all is meaningless and void of reason is itself a creation of meaning out of the void motivated by the very void of reason. The process of forming meaning, it seems, can perhaps not be escaped, even by one the greatest so-called nihilists. Perhaps, then, Cioran never really declared true nihilism.

There is a more obvious reading of Cioran that can reasonably come off as if it were created by someone who outright hates life and lives with a constant bitterness toward everyone and everything. But there is also another reading that reveals a paradoxical reverence and embrace of life. Although Cioran might not have explicitly agreed with this, to speak of life with such candor in the way he did, to think it is worthy to be spoken of at all, to refuse to lie to it or about it despite how dark or bleak it might be, perhaps suggests a hidden but deep admiration and acceptance of it. When asked once why he wrote about such dismal topics in the way he did, Cioran said, "Everything that is formulated becomes more tolerable." Time and time again, his work demonstrated this, revealing the perhaps vile and horribly unresolvable qualities of life, while simultaneously reveling in the potential for redemption contained in them—a worthiness of enduring, of thinking, of writing, of living life. Cursed with the gift of consciousness, we are all inescapably forced into a beautiful confrontation of the void and the absurd inevitability of creating meaning and somethingness out of it.

Cioran's work is likely not for everyone, but for those to whom it appeals, it is likely to a great degree. As all art and literature arguably should, his work attempts to reflect with as much brute earnestness as possible on the things most of us know and feel but are often too scared or unsure to either discuss or contemplate. He was one of the rare explorers willing, or perhaps forced, to travel through the depths of hell and the heights of despair and then tell of it. Cioran's work can be seen simply as a collection of life-denying nihilistic thoughts, or it can also be seen as an embodiment of the irrational but no less potent force of human creative consciousness at work—and its ability to meaningfully endure even its own horrible conditions. And in this—in his works' arguably successful confrontation and embrace of the sad, hopeless, and absurd parts of life—they serve as enduring and important connection points to these often hidden but deeply shared human experiences, reminding us that we aren't so alone and reassuring us with the comforting notion that "[We are] simply an accident. Why take it all so seriously?"

DON'T WATER IT DOWN

The Philosophy of Franz Kafka

Franz Kafka is regarded as one of the greatest literary figures in recent history. He is known for his uniquely dark, disorienting, and surreal writing style—a style and quality so particular to him that anything that resembles it has come to be known as *Kafkaesque*.

Kafka was born in Prague in 1883 to Herman and Julie Kafka. His father was a well-to-do businessman who, through sheer force of will and a brash, aggressive personality, managed to rise from the working class, build a successful business, marry a well-educated woman, and become a member of the upper-middle class. As parents tend to do, Herman hoped for a child that would measure up to his ideal of a person. Franz Kafka was not that. Franz was born a small, anxious, and sickly boy, and he mostly remained that way. As a result, through no fault of his own, Franz would become a great source of disappointment for his father and a sort of psychological punching bag for him as he attempted to mold Franz into who he wished he was but could never be.

Throughout his adolescence, Franz developed an urge to write as a means of dealing with his increasing sense of anxiety, guilt, and self-hatred. Of course, his father did not allow him to pursue writing and ultimately defined the borders of Kafka's life, forcing him to pursue law as a profession instead.

During his time studying law in college, Kafka continued writing and met one of his only real friends, Max Brod, another writer who would eventually convince Kafka to publish his first three collections of work. These pieces sold very poorly, though, and essentially went unnoticed.

After college, Kafka would go on to work in a law office, and then for an insurance company. Here, Kafka would become subject to long hours, unpaid overtime, massive amounts of paperwork, and absurd, complex bureaucratic systems. Kafka was understandably miserable. While working at the insurance company, Kafka continued writing on the side, producing some of his most notable pieces, including *The Trial*, *The Castle*, and *Amerika*. He did not attempt to publish any of these at the time, however, and even left much of his work unfinished. Kafka continued working at the insurance company for the majority of his remaining short life, while also continuing to write around his work schedule. In 1924, he died of tuberculosis at age forty-one. With exception to the few initial story collections, he never published any of his writing during his lifetime nor did he ever receive any recognition for the small amount he did. He died believing that his work wasn't any good. On his death bed, he even instructed Max Brod to burn all of his unpublished manuscripts following his death. Obviously, Brod did not follow Kafka's instructions—and here we are, about one hundred years later, talking about him.

After Kafka died, Brod spent the following year or so working to organize and publish Kafka's notes and manuscripts. Over the following decade, Kafka would become one of the most prominent literary and philosophical figures of the twentieth century. In other words, one of the greatest writers and thinkers of the century lived his life with his work buried in some drawer, aware, unaware, or indifferent to the fact that he was sitting on some the most significant works in modern history. He was, in the eyes of his father, an inadequate disappointment—and yet, in the eyes of history, he is an immensely important individual. One can only wonder how many individuals like Kafka have walked and continue to walk this earth, completely disconnected or restricted from ever seeing who they really are or could be. How many *Kafkas* have lived and died without ever sharing their voice with the world; voices that would have changed it forever? How many people never know who they'll be after they're gone?

Fortunately for everyone other than Kafka, his work was saved, and an entirely new term came into being to define the style and focus of his writing: Kafkaesque.

Generally, the term Kafkaesque refers to the bureaucratic nature of capitalistic, judicial, and government systems—the sort of complex, unclear processes in which no one individual ever really has a comprehensive grasp of what is going on, and the system doesn't really care. But the quality of Kafkaesque also seems to extend much further than this. It is not necessarily exemplified merely by what these systems are, but rather, by the reaction of the individuals subjected to them, as well as what this might represent.

In one of Kafka's most famous novels, *The Trial*, the protagonist Josef K. is suddenly arrested at his home one morning. The officers do not inform Joseph of why he is being arrested, and he is forced through a long, absurd trial in which nothing is really explained or makes much sense. The trial is riddled with corruption and disorderliness, and by the end of the novel, after having meandered through the entire thing, Josef is never told why he was arrested, and yet, he remains guilty of the crime he is charged with.

In another one of his popular stories, *Metamorphosis*, the protagonist Gregor Samsa awakens to discover that he has been turned into an insect, with no explanation. The recurring issues that Gregor faces throughout the novel involve getting to work, dealing with his boss, and providing financially for his inconsiderately needy family. Gregor, of course, cannot do any of this. He is a bug. And so, he experiences increased dread trying to deal with his situation while becoming a useless nuisance to his family.

In both stories, the protagonists are faced with sudden, absurd circumstances. There are no explanations. And, in the end, there is no real chance of overcoming it. They are outmatched by the arbitrary, senseless obstacles they face—in part, because they can't even understand or control any of what is happening. The crux of Kafka's work seems to be the tension created by this confrontation with the absurd—a conflict in which a character's efforts, reasoning, and sense of the world are met with an inescapable senselessness. The Kafkaesque quality is found in the characters' impossible struggles to make sense of what's happening to them and how to resolve their situations, wherein success is both impossible and, in the end, ultimately pointless. And yet, they try anyway.

One interpretation is that these circumstances are emblematic of Kafka's take on the human condition, which could be characterized as the unyielding desire for answers about and conquest of the existential problems of anxiety, guilt, absurdity, and suffering, paired with an inability to ever really understand or control the source of these problems and effectively overcome them. But the kicker, and perhaps most important part is that, even in the face of absurd, despairing circumstances, Kafka's characters don't give up. At least initially, they continue on and fight against their situations, trying to reason, understand, or work their way out of the senselessness. But in the end, it is ultimately to no avail. Perhaps in this, Kafka is suggesting that the struggle to find solace and understanding is both inescapable and impossible. As conscious, rational beings, we fight against the absurdity, trying to resolve the discrepancy between us and the universe. But ironically, we only serve to perpetuate the very struggle we are trying to resolve by trying to resolve the unresolvable. And in this sense, on some level, we almost want the struggle.

Of course, this is just one interpretation. Ultimately, because of its vague, surreal, and inexplicable quality, Kafka's work lends itself to nearly as many interpretations as readers. Perhaps the idea is that we shouldn't take our absurd condition so seriously. Perhaps the idea is we should and must struggle against it. Or perhaps the idea is that we can't know what the idea is. In truth, only Kafka will ever have known exactly what his work meant, and it's fair to speculate that in some sense, perhaps not even him. What is undeniable, though, is that Kafka's work has left a lasting impact on literature, philosophy, and humanity at large. It has helped readers around the world feel less alone in their own hunches of truth and moments of Kafkaesque experience. Kafka's own story is not necessarily unusual. Neither the cruelty of his father nor the sadness of his life are that uncommon. To have been born into a faulty family, a bad place in the world, or a weak body or brain; to live and die having never recognized one's potential; to have been stuck in a bureaucratic cog of a business organization or government system; to have felt the guilt and anxiety of existence for no clear reason; we have all, at least at times, experienced the Kafkaesque. Kafka's work is not considered great because it describes something profoundly unique but because it describes something common in a profound way—an encapsulation of an often-indescribable experience of life that touches us all.

When referring to Kafka, writer Anne Rice once said that his work helped her realize the following approach in her own work: "Don't bend; don't water it down; don't try to make it logical; don't edit your own soul according to the fashion. Rather, follow your most intense obsessions mercilessly." Kafka's work sought not to alleviate the soul through remedies of false hope or delusion, but rather, through the direct confrontation with the darker aspects of life. By distorting reality to map more accurately onto his own sense of human experience, he revealed a certain remedy of unhindered self-examination and carved out a place in the world for others to do the same. In a letter to a friend, Kafka wrote:

> I think we ought to read only the kind of books that wound or stab us. If the book we're reading doesn't wake us up with a blow to the head, what are we reading for? So that it will make us happy . . . Good Lord, we would be happy precisely if we had no books.

Kafka's work embodies and reminds us, not that we wish to give up, but that despite all the problems, we wish to continue. We wish to struggle against the universe and forge our own way. We wish to honestly confront and connect over the absurd, however hard it may be.

DEALING WITH AN EXISTENTIAL CRISIS

The Philosophy of Jean-Paul Sartre

We are born into this world without choosing—without choosing to be born, without choosing the parents we are born to, our location in time and space we are born at, the bodies we are born into, and all the rest. As we open our eyes, we peer out at a world moving around us—a world that we had no say in. And soon, to paraphrase existentialist philosopher Jean-Paul Sartre, we will begin to face the problem of *choosing what we do with what's been done to us*.

Jean-Paul Sartre is one of the most widely recognized and cited thinkers of *existentialism*, a movement of thinking that took form during the nineteenth century, initially fashioned by individuals like Søren Kierkegaard, Friedrich Nietzsche, and Fyodor Dostoevsky, and then further popularized by individuals including Albert Camus, Martin Heidegger, and, of course, Sartre.

In Sartre's lecture, *Existentialism is a Humanism*, he famously summarized the primary principle of existentialism with the line: "Existence precedes essence." Essence, here, means the qualities of a thing that create its purpose. For example, Sartre referenced how a paper knife is designed with a specific purpose in mind before it is made, and only once it is given a predetermined purpose and designed accordingly, is it manufactured into being; in which case, its essence precedes its existence. With the exception of itself, humanity does this with nearly everything it makes. As rational beings, we create things for reasons. Even if the reason is to make the point that we can create things for no reason, we have merely found ourselves in the paradox of creating for the reason of having none. We exist with the innate desire for reasons—reasons for what we do, who we are, why we are, and so on. And here lies the beginning of our existential problem.

According to Sartre and many others, there is no predetermined meaning or reason to human life. There is no authority figure designing us or our lives. And there is no essence to our existence prior to our existence. Rather, life exists for itself. Beyond itself, it is intrinsically meaningless. Whenever we confront this potential realization—that the nature of life, including our self, appears not to agree with reason—we can often find ourselves in a sort of existential crisis. However, Sartre and the existentialists don't see this as despairing, but rather, freeing.

If we are not made with a specific purpose prior to existence, we create our purpose through our existence. In other words, through the choices we make and the actions we take in life, we create who we are and what life means. "Man," Sartre said, "is nothing else but what he purposes, he exists only in so far as he realises himself, he is therefore nothing else but the sum of his actions, nothing else but what his life is." The byproduct of this, of life's inherent meaninglessness, is an inherent freedom: the freedom to choose who we are, how we live, and what matters to us. And here we experience the next rung of our existential problem: the anxiety or anguish of choice.

With essentially an infinite potential number of choices and combinations of choices for how to live and think and be, the anxiety of choosing properly can be difficult to bear. Ironically though, the choice we make here—in reaction to the anxiety of choice—is perhaps the most important choice of all.

The easier, knee-jerk response to the anxiety of choice is simply just not choosing: to mindlessly assimilate popular, common templates and ideas of life, follow standard routes of belief and purpose already laid down for us, and deflect nearly all the responsibility of choice onto others and the circumstances of our life. Sartre referred to this as *bad faith*—a form of lying to ourselves and denying our basic freedom. In other words, a short-term attempt to dampen the anxiety of being that in turn costs us our true self and our authentic sense of the world. Even choosing to not choose is still a choice. There is no escaping the requirements of choice. This is perhaps the fundamental existential choice: to choose or not to choose. In this choice, one either harnesses the anguish of human freedom or relinquishes it, either builds a life of intention or lives a life of complacency.

We each have our little flickers of time here. No one else will ever know much, if anything, of what it's like to be who we are. And for the most part, no one will ever really care. Our life is ultimately our life, and so long as we are not harming others in the process, we must create a life of our own meaning, determining our own objects of importance, committing to their pursuit, and reaping the significance and wonder of life along the way.

Truthfully, we seldom have enough information to properly make any choice, including how much we might agree with Sartre or anyone else. Throughout our life, we are faced with serious decisions about what we believe, who we are, and what we do—and mostly none of it is self-evident. If we look, we will always find a reason to regret any decision we make. Move or stay; agree or disagree; take the job or quit; marry or divorce; walk one path or another; in all cases, whatever the choice may be, we will only ever know the outcome of the one we take. And no path that we take will ever ultimately resolve the uncertainty of life.

However, perhaps it is less about getting a potential course of life right and more about attempting to do so with self-honesty and virtue—to live a life that can be looked back on with the knowledge that some of our decisions were perhaps wrong in their effects but right in their intention not to sell ourselves short.

It is, of course, all incredibly hard and complicated, but the challenge found in this—in the whirlpool of uncertainty, absurdity, and responsibility—is perhaps the unavoidable price of the great gift that we all are given at birth. But it is just that: a gift. To face up to the abyss, to feel the anguish of choice and potentiality, to bear the weight of self—all are but visceral, humbling, and beautiful reminders of the potency of life running through our veins. Perhaps our only job is to realize this and make the gift worth its price. Whether you agree with Sartre or not, ultimately, his ideas are a reminder to do just that.

No matter what we do or say or believe, there will always be a great many people who disagree or judge or ridicule or become upset by our decisions, but so long as we are not intentionally harming anyone else, it is of essential importance that we try as often as possible to ensure that among those people, our self is not one of them.

EMBRACE THE ABSURD

The Philosophy of Albert Camus

At any street corner, the feeling of absurdity can strike any man in the face.

Albert Camus

Albert Camus was a twentieth-century French-Algerian writer and philosopher most commonly associated with the existentialism movement. Specifically, within this school of thought, Camus was a proponent of the idea that our relationship with the universe is completely and fundamentally absurd. What makes Camus' insight highly unique and helpful in this matter is the way in which he wrestled with this concept, what he called *the absurd*, or man's inescapably paradoxical relationship with the universe, and arguably, that he came out victorious.

What makes something absurd, in the mind of Camus, can be best be described with his following analogy:

> If I see a man armed only with a sword attack a group of machine guns, I shall consider his act to be absurd. But it is so solely by virtue of the disproportion between his intention and the reality he will encounter, of the contradiction I notice between his true strength and the aim he has in view . . . from the simplest to the most complex, the magnitude of the absurdity will be in direct ratio to the distance between the two terms of my comparison .
> . . The absurd is essentially a divorce. It lies in neither of the elements compared; it is born of their confrontation.

In other words, neither the human nor the universe are necessarily absurd on their own, but rather, their relationship is absurd. As humans, we exist with an innate desire for meaning, reason, and order, but yet, we simultaneously exist in a universe that appears to lack all of the above. So far as we can tell, the universe is completely indifferent. Thus, what we want and expect from the universe is fundamentally in contradiction with what we get. In this conflict, the absurdity of the human experience is found. However, despite this realization, Camus rejects the nihilistic hopelessness that might sound like a reasonable conclusion, and instead, provokes the absurdity of life as a means of finding worthy and potent experience within it. For Camus, to become aware of and accept the absurdity of life is to transcend it. We may live strange, absurd lives in an indifferent universe, but rather than hopelessness, despair, or worst of all, suicide, we should accept life's absurdity, make it our own, and overcome it.

In his essay, *The Myth of Sisyphus*, Camus references the Greek story of Sisyphus as a powerful allegory and teaching to overcome life's absurdity. In the story, as a punishment for trying to outsmart the gods, the Greek king Sisyphus is condemned to roll a giant rock up a hill. As part of the punishment, however, every time Sisyphus gets to the top of the hill, the rock rolls back down to the bottom, forcing him to start again, over and over, for all of eternity.

For absolutely no reason, Sisyphus rolls this rock up the hill, only to watch it roll back down, again and again. In this, Camus draws a connection between the tiresome and futile fate of Sisyphus and the human experience. However, Camus wrote, "One must imagine Sisyphus happy." With this, Camus makes the hopeful yet reasonable assertion that even in the ordinary, repetitive, absurd, and futile experiences of our life, we can and should still find worthy experience and happiness.

For Camus, there are plenty of tremendous reasons to endure the potential absurdity and pointlessness of rolling the rock up and down the hill. All of the things that exist around the rock that tend to seem as though they are less important than getting the rock to the top of the hill—the sun, the trees, the refreshing breeze, the friends, the relationships, the family, the art, the self-exploration, and anything else we can find interesting and wondrous—are, for Camus, all there is, and all there needs to be. These things are not the background, but rather, they are the foreground.

Furthermore, it is the absurdity of these things that allows them to have the potential for intrigue and wonder. And it is up to us to be conscious of this and derive meaning from them all.

Unlike anything else in the known universe, we are able to consciously observe, consider, reason, and act. As a result of our unique abilities, we ask ourselves *why*. We desperately try to find the answer. We get increasingly clever in our attempts, yet every time, just like the rock in *The Myth of Sisyphus*, at some point, we return to the bottom of the hill, leaving us to start anew. As a result of this constant inability to satiate our desire for ultimate meaning and truth, we can often find ourselves drudging over the seeming absurdity and futility of it all. However, Camus felt that even in the conflict of absurdity, we can be ok and still live happy lives.

In the acceptance of our absurd human experience, we realize that the point is not to eliminate absurdity or find and defend some ultimate truth, but rather, it is to be conscious and appreciative of the things within the absurdity—to look for, find, and create things that are interesting and personally meaningful. Furthermore, Camus suggested that in recognizing our absurdity, we can better accept and share value with the people around us because we can understand that we are all struggling victims of *the absurd*.

For Camus, continuing on in life and using its absurdity as a means of virtue, exploration, art, and unique experience is perhaps the highest and most worthy achievement. It is thus the absurdity of life that makes it worth living in the first place. When referencing the predicament of Sisyphus's fate, Camus wrote, "The struggle itself towards the heights is enough to fill a man's heart."

PART III

THE PROBLEM OF OTHER PEOPLE

Throughout my life, I have explored various aspects of philosophy and science, all driven by the self-oriented goal to better understand who I am, why am I, and how to better be me. Ironically, one of the most important things I have learned is how to be less self-oriented. I am, without doubt, far from complete or virtuously accomplished in this goal, but nonetheless, I still think it is one of the greatest benefits of contemplating philosophical ideas. As you do so, and inevitably descend down into the cavernous realm of meaninglessness, darkness, and absurdity, where even the trivial things in life become complicated and hard to see, you grasp more plainly and candidly the truth of who we are as a people. Understanding more about yourself is, in some significant way, understanding more about others. I have personally found this to be true time and time again. Every time I reflect on the absurdity of my existence or discover a new idea about the potential mechanisms of it, I only become more aware and forgiving of those I love, dislike, and will never know.

What use is finding or creating meaning in life if you cannot maintain and share it well with others? What use is it to understand how you or the world (maybe) works if every time you encounter someone else it throws everything off? Is it even possible to live well without being able to live well with others (in at least some sense)? The following essays take on these questions; questions that help us to understand the problem of other people.

EVERYONE IS TRAPPED IN AN ABSURD RELATIONSHIP WITH EVERYTHING

people are tired
strafed by life
mutilated either by love or no love.

. . .

people are not good to each other one on one.
people are just not good to each other.

we are afraid.
we think that hatred signifies strength.
that punishment is love.

Charles Bukowski

I t takes no more than a dog barking a little too long or
a person moving around a little too loudly while we
are in a wretched mood that we didn't choose, to feel a
visceral reminder of the non-rhythmic disorder always

around and in us, to feel a world that is propelled and shared with innumerable other beings, all wanting it to sound and move as if it were their own just as much as we do, all struggling over such an impossibility.

We know we aren't the center of everything. We learned that, hopefully, sometime in very early adolescence. However, despite this, each inevitable disillusioning experience can inject us with a sense that we have been singled out, that we have personally and intentionally been given a misery or frustration that requires blame or answer. Of course, some of the time, this is the case. But how often do we confuse the faults of existence in general with the faults of other people and things specifically? How often do we confuse the anxiety and confusion and plight of all humankind with our own?

Everyone is experiencing the same dissonance of being, living their own story through the nauseating rollercoaster of ups and downs to nowhere. It is both banal and almost hollow to say that we should be compassionate and kind to others because of this. Every first-grade child knows this in fewer words. The notion of togetherness and compassion is sold to us in soda and fast-food commercials as well as nearly every Disney movie. It is so commodified, clichéd, and obvious that it's hard to even take seriously the idea of needing to consider it further. Life isn't a soda commercial nor a Disney movie, and it isn't anywhere near as clean as a first-grade child could likely even imagine. There is a world filled with malevolence and anger and greed and

impatience and all the rest. But for this very reason—
because compassion is so trite and yet still seemingly so
hard and absent—it is perhaps all the more essential
and rational to give it serious focus and effort.

Although it can, and at times almost certainly
should be, compassion need not be synonymous with
what might generally be considered agreeableness.
Rather, the compassion being referred to here suggests
a sympathetic understanding of others' lack of agreeableness—an awareness serving to help calibrate our
easily incited impatience, anger, finger-pointing, or
disdain toward others over mostly nothing, or things
that we don't really know or understand.

There is a suffering and confusion a part of existence that we all know and feel yet seem to so often
struggle to grant others. To not see the so obviously
unobvious thing behind everything, to hate, to seek
vengeance, to frequently act on anger, to declare certainty in almost anything, all contradict the very struggle and confusion of life that bring us so much pain
in the first place. How often do we turn minor incon-
veniences into major ones due to this lack of consideration? Or worse yet, how often do we turn tragedies
of random circumstance into tragedies of hatred? It's
not that one should not be annoyed by or disagree
with another person or group—nor is it the case that
we should not try to work for what we believe in or
against what we disagree with. But it is perhaps worth
approaching every instance, as often as we can, with
the awareness that the ignorance and annoyance and

sometimes cruelty that we find in others is sometimes found by others in us, sometimes at the same time and with equally valid reasons. Who is right in such cases? Perhaps in some of them, no one is—perhaps not even the person who thinks they've overcome the problem by realizing it's happening and determining that they are superior to both parties by realizing how foolish both are. Even here, if one acts in such a way, one is exhibiting a conceit and smugness over others by thinking that they have understood the foolishness of being conceited and smug. Everyone is absurd in their attempt to trump their own absurd relationship with everything—and all the more so when we do not realize that we, even here, are also a part of everyone. There is but one thing that seems to have any positive effect against such absurdity: a sort of compassion for the whole. We must try to remember that everyone is in it, and everyone is flailing against it for the same reasons as everyone else. Thus, within limits perhaps, everyone deserves such consideration and compassion.

Of course, there are actions and people that warrant harsh scrutiny and proper handling. Like all things, there are cases that reside further out on the periphery where the lines become blurrier and the responses less obvious. But it could be argued that a certain compassion is still applicable even if a conflicting response is necessary.

Ultimately, there is a movement in this world with no one in the driver's seat. Everyone is dealt different, complex hands of good and bad luck, all of which causes everyone to be who they are and aren't. At bottom, no one chooses who they are born as, and no one chooses everything that happens thereafter, but ultimately, everything forms what one is. In the words of Schopenhauer, "Man can do what he wills but he cannot will what he wills."

None of this is to make light of the colossal difficulty in accomplishing such compassion. Being not only aware of but also acting in accordance with this ideal demands an incredibly hard and constant effort, most likely impossible in the complete sense. And because it's so hard, a great number of people don't. And because a great number of people don't, it only becomes exponentially harder. For most, if not all of us, this compassion is an ember that is perpetually on the brink of burning out. But most, if not all of us, are constantly teetering in and out of being the one that is in need of compassion and understanding. And with every insight and consideration, with every moment of self-reflection and temperance, there is an opportunity to influence a slight change in the cycle, even if it's just in us. It is a profound, noble act of humanity to use our awareness of our unawareness as a source of compassion and understanding for others and ourselves, as opposed to a source of disdain and bitterness—to use our unique conscious position to know how hard it is to be in a conscious position, and to acknowledge that everyone else is, in fact, also in one.

REALITY IS JUST AN ILLUSION WE ALL AGREE ON

At some point in all of our timelines, the lights turned on for the very first time. It isn't clear exactly when or what it was like because that first moment of complex consciousness has long since lapsed in our memory. But at some point, everything began to become some form of everything for the first time. The world (or rather, our mental construct of the world) began. And in this birth from nothingness into our subjective color of everything, we became both the creator and the object of our worldview.

"We see the world not as it is, but as we are," wrote twentieth-century author Anaïs Nin. Inexorably bound to it, our view, experience, and understanding of everything is created by our unique, personal interior experience, which is created by our consciousness, which is created by the natural world, all in a reflexive, continual feedback loop. And so, the world *as it actually is* exists in some major part behind a veil of our subjectivity. This is not to suggest the solipsistic stance that the physical world does not exist outside of consciousness, but that the particular image of the world we experience does not.

Ultimately, we are in something that we can only touch through a body and know through a conscious mind, forever prohibited from contacting it outside of our personally filtered experience of it, and forever condemned to the persistent illusions or hallucinations that might come as a result. For good reason, likely this exact reason, a distinct quality of our form of consciousness is its ability and desire to inquire about and into itself and the world. It wants to know what things really are, how they are, and why they are. It wants to dig and dig and dig until it hits the innermost core and knows all there is to know, finally able to understand and control the mechanisms of existence and free itself from the necessity of further inquisition. But what if, in fact, there is no such core to be reached, or there is, but it cannot be reached by us?

Of course, there are plenty of things we can *know* and be right about in plenty of different contexts. I can point to a blue pillow and say that the pillow is blue, and since most of us have eyeballs, optic nerves, occipital lobes, and human brains that generally function the same way when it comes to visual processing, we can agree that I am right. However, we can't *actually know* that what we see is the same blue, because we cannot see into each others' minds. Although we both agree we see blue, we cannot know if we are actually having the same mental experience, or *qualia*, of what we are calling blue. This and all other problems related to the disconnect between our perception and what is really outside of our mind is known as the *egocentric predicament*. This problem is made even more difficult when trying to understand what is experienced in other people's minds, which is the concept known as the *explanatory gap*. And so, even here in this simple, everyday example, we cannot confirm that anybody is objectively right. Furthermore, someone who is severely color blind might not agree that the pillow is even any type of blue at all. To them, if they do agree, they must agree not out of their own experience, but out of a willingness to sacrifice the truth of what they see for what the majority of people see and tell them. But fundamentally, are they really wrong if they say the pillow isn't blue? What if all humans were color blind? Or, what if the pillow were in fact a much more vibrant color of some other wavelength that we can't even imagine, let alone perceive? Wouldn't we all, who say it's blue, be just as right or wrong as the colorblind individual who says it isn't? This is all to say that even though there can be *derivative truths* concluded from sufficiently shared subjective experiences, about which one can be right (i.e., that the pillow is blue), in the very same sentiment at the very same time, the same someone can be fundamentally wrong. And if somehow, suddenly, we could all perceive different wavelengths of color, and we all agreed that the pillow was in fact not blue, then we would all also agree that anyone who still said it was would be wrong, even though the pillow itself never changed.

How many things in the conceptual atmosphere of politics, morality, economics, metaphysics, and so forth are blue pillows? What are we all color blind to? And what have we all agreed is true simply and only because we all agree that it's true? What is underneath all the different shades of blue, green, red, and so on? This is not to say that such agreements of perception and value judgments aren't majorly useful and sufficient in many if not most cases, but it is to point out the off-putting malleability and abstractness of everything we think is true.

There are, of course, ways of measuring physical reality through tools and methods that might be able to supersede any sort of perceptual illusions, biases, and so forth. But also of course, all tools must start and end through the first and final tool of the human mind. There is no way out of the mind, and thus, there is no way into the world as it actually is. And moreover, it would seem that if we could understand and explain what all the physical stuff of the material world is and how it came to be, we still wouldn't necessarily be any better off knowing what it means. And so, if all human truths are based on agreements of shared subjective, internal experiences, which are all limited inexorably by human perception, then we can likely never know if there even is a core of objective truth to be reached, or, if there is, if we can conclusively ever reach it. And if this is the case, then would we not, in every effort toward such a goal of fundamental axiomatic conclusions of reality and truth, be endeavoring to achieve the impossible? And consequently, is not attempting to think and talk in generally true, objective terms also impossible? Not useless, but impossible in the absolute sense. If we cannot arrive at any grand, fundamental, objective truths in life, but we must build all conclusions, ideas, and discourse on top of some sort of sufficiently shared subjective foundation, then this places discussion, thinking, and believing on a constantly shifting, unstable, and wide-spanning ground of various types of subjective, ideological worldviews. This absurdity is at the core of all worldviews, spiderwebbing out into the attempts to discuss and think about even relatively commonplace ideas. This phenomenon potentially reveals itself when we confront another person who is so obviously wrong but has no idea how they could possibly be so, while at the same time being equally certain that we are so obviously wrong, even though we have no idea how we could possibly be so. Or perhaps when we confront a sudden breakdown of what we were so sure about for so long, realizing that everything we believe, individually or collectively, is in fact entirely the opposite of what is now apparently true. This is learning if it ends, but some kind of madness if it never does.

Of course, it is obligatory to mention that all of the aforementioned ideas could themselves be wrong. They might entirely oppose what you believe or feel you know to be true. But, ironically, if anything, that would seem to support the main point here.

In all cases, for the most part, knowing what the real color of things are (metaphorically speaking) is perhaps minimally relevant to living and thriving as an individual and as a species. Perhaps what matters more is that we can agree and disagree on subjective things sufficiently well enough, cordially enough, and often enough. And it seems as though that in order to do so, if such a feat is possible, the prerequisite is a willingness to embrace often being wrong.

Naturally and culturally, the desire to be right is a deeply enduring and forceful one. As often as possible, sometimes at all costs and despite good reason, we are both compelled by our psyche and pressured by our social world to always be right. And when we aren't, it hurts—so much so that it can often create horrible sensations in the brain akin to that of real physical pain. And so, we try to avoid it (or at least avoid admitting it)—and yet, it is impossible to avoid. Furthermore, it is possibly the case that fundamentally we are never actually right at all. In the words of St. Augustine, "I err, therefore I am." As a consciousness in the form that we are born into, we are all put up against the imperative of our mind's desire for absolute truth, while simultaneously living in a world that prohibits us from obtaining it. We will all cling to reasons and answers and worldviews only to have them smashed to pieces time and time again, whether we know it or admit it to ourselves or not. We will all not only be wrong often, but right rarely, even in the meta, subjective sense. And so, perhaps if we wish to be ok with consciousness, we must learn how to be ok with this. Perhaps we must learn how to fundamentally be ok with being wrong, or we will loathe ourselves until the end. Perhaps we must love and accept the hypocrisy that runs through the very veins of the human condition, or we will hate all of humankind. Perhaps we must learn how to dial back our expectations and the degree to which we dread the inevitable failure of everything we believe, and the beliefs of others just the same. This is not to make light of the immense challenge of such an arduous endeavor. It is an endless, upward climb of surpassing one's default mode and understanding of the world. But perhaps if we can, at least some of the time, succeed in doing so, we can feel a little less embarrassed, disgusted, miserable, ashamed, bitter, angry, and all the rest. And perhaps we can be a little less wrong a little more often.

HOW TO REMAIN CALM(ER) WITH PEOPLE

There are so many reasons to be angry. We live in a culture that makes idealism its goal and a world that makes idealism impossible. There is so much wrong—with others, with our self, with the way things are. We reside somewhere inside a brain, watching and feeling its fervent, insatiable efforts to try and make the world go its way; and every day, with as little as the sound of a car horn or a lost set of keys, we are reminded that this is an impossibility: that we are stuck between the awareness of a god and the temperament of an animal. Often anger just makes a lot of sense.

Of course, there are different types of anger, different instances and sources, and different temperaments with different propensities toward it. And arguably, in many cases, anger can be a very useful emotion. It can be a source of insight into when we've been wronged, when things are going poorly, and when we want change. It can be a source of character, of creativity, of motivation, and of strength. But in other cases, arguably far more often, it can also be a source of foolishness, of miscalculation, of regret, of resentment, and of detachment—from others and from ourselves.

We so often take personally what the world does without us in mind. Certainly, we can be wronged in ways that are unjust, targeted, correctable, or preventable—and in these cases, anger can and likely should be used as a source of motivation to recognize this, stand up, and defend ourselves. But arguably, more often we are wronged by the world in ways that no amount of angered force will help correct or solve. Human existence is so unbelievably absurd and chaotic and strange, it is a wonder that it works in our favor at all any of the time. We are lodged inside a clump of soft tissue that we don't even understand, experiencing a reality made of particles that we can't perceive, all made and governed by a universe that operates in chaotic contradiction to the meaningful order we so desperately desire—the very same desire the universe forced onto us. We were set up, destined to have everything fall over and over. We can tend to resist and reject any sort of softer acceptance and sadness in response to this, and instead, many of us can become callused over with a sort of brute and frequent anger. This has its place and purpose, but at a certain point, like a callus on the hand, we can become numb and unfeeling, making us less able to properly know and deal with the true conditions of our circumstances. Those who are often angered reveal themselves to be a strange sort of optimist, still in denial of the tragedies of this life and the death of their youthful innocence—the belief that life can be what it can't. Despite all evidence, we are, if we are this, in some non-traditional way, still hopeful—hopeful that things should and will go in our favor most of the time. And thus, we are constantly angered by life's incongruency. We become angry about everything because we refuse to let ourselves be sad about some things.

A theory in psychology known as appraisal theory, initially developed by psychologist Magda Arnold, suggests that our emotional responses are in large part created by our conscious evaluations of events—how we view, interpret, and label stimuli rather than the stimuli themselves. In other words, in between our primary experience of an event and our emotional experience of an event, there is a filtering process that occurs through and is based on our cognitive faculties. In this space, how we think based on our experiences, perceptions, views, and values determines what we feel. For example, if we have a fondness for cats and believe that cats are sweet and harmless, seeing or holding one will likely be a favorable emotional experience. However, for someone who believes cats to be threatening or devious, this experience will likely be a negative one. The emotional responses will be completely different while the stimulus remains exactly the same. Of course, since our emotions are so wide-ranging, complicated, and partly rooted in consciousness (a topic largely uncracked by science), a comprehensive understanding of our emotions is still yet to be seen, and appraisal theory remains just that: a theory. And even in the case that this theory is correct, some of our appraisals will still be more unconscious and immediate than others, making them harder if not potentially impossible to get into and control—and perhaps sometimes for good reason. However, it is still fair to argue that in many cases that are often more common, the concept suggested by appraisal theory has immense value and practical use. Especially when we are angered frequently or remain angered for long, drawn-out periods of time, there is likely large opportunity to change out our mental filter in favor of better, more productive emotional experiences. In the words of American author David Foster Wallace:

> Learning how to think really means learning how to exercise some control over how and what you think. It means being conscious and aware enough to choose what you pay attention to and to choose how you construct meaning from experience. Because if you cannot or will not exercise this kind of choice . . . you will be totally hosed.

This idea also coincides with principles central to the philosophy of stoicism. For the stoics, events in the world are objective and neutral, and our qualitative emotional experiences are merely a product of the narratives we tell ourselves. "It doesn't hurt me unless I interpret it's happening as harmful to me. I can choose not to," wrote Marcus Aurelius.

Perhaps what we need, then, during those moments of opportunity to reflect mindfully on events and determine our evaluations, is to inject healthy but sufficient doses of a sort of pessimism and compassion. When we believe the world is congenial and manageable in some just way, when we think we are at the center of all things and all events in the world that happen to us happen at us, when we neglect to consider that suffering and ignorance are fundamental to all people, anger can and likely will eat us alive. Rather, if we realize that the world has not singled us out, that most people are good people trying their best, that ignorance is far more often behind the curtain and not malice, that our emotions are not the result of being made victims by others but by us not taking ownership of them ourselves, that life is inherently difficult and suffering is fundamental to everyone, we can perhaps more accurately evaluate if what we are angered by is worthy of being angry about, and how.

Of course, none of this is to say that we should live an agreeable life in which our anger is always denied its expression. Nor is it to say that we shouldn't have expectations and make an effort to control and react to circumstances to the best of our ability. But it is to say that often anger comes from a place that isn't angry about the thing we seem to be angry about, that anger is often a liability and not an asset, and that we aren't locked in to falling victim to it by always letting ourselves think that we have personally been made victims by the world. In the words of

Marcus Aurelius, "Understand at last that you have something in you more powerful and divine than what causes the bodily passions and pulls you like a mere puppet."

All of this might sound perfectly reasonable, useful, and insightful, but of course, that is until you get angry. It is then that all of this sounds impossible, nonsensical, cheap, or trite; but perhaps it is then and for this reason especially that these ideas matter so much—the fact that we can become so detached from our faculties of reason and wisdom, and that anger can take us so far from what we truly think and want.

PART IV

THE DEVELOPMENT OF SELF

To live well is to live authentically. This is easy to say and agree with, but I have found that the most difficult part of any concept pertaining to selfhood is actually acting it out. Knowing how to know and be yourself versus actually knowing and being it is like knowing the mechanics of how to surf on paper and then going out into the ocean and encountering an actual wave. These are not the same. And so, one must practice the mechanics of selfhood and take actual steps toward actualizing it in the world.

Admittedly, I have and continue to find this practice vague and difficult. I believe it is likely a constant effort that will only end when I do. I don't feel that I fully know my *true self*. I don't know if I am convinced that I have a true self that I can ever fully know. I don't know what I am fully motivated by. And I don't know how I can ever confirm if I do know any of these things. But I do think this is a good place to start. In the same way that wisdom about the world begins with knowing you know nothing, *wisdom of the self* begins with knowing you know, at the very least, very little about who you really are.

I believe that *self-discovery* is perhaps one of the great tasks and challenges of human life and deriving personal meaning from it—discovering who we are while living in a world that constantly tries to change us and a brain that never clearly discloses to us who we actually are and why. The following essays cover topics, ideas, and thinkers that have helped me grapple with this convoluted objective. They have aided me in better assessing the perplexity of who I am and provided me with reminders as to how and why I ought to be me as best I can, as often as I can.

A REASON TO STOP WORRYING WHAT OTHERS THINK

Somewhere inside your head, somewhere inside the seemingly impossible organization of electrically charged meat that calls itself the brain, is *you*. Neither you nor anyone else properly understands how this *you* comes to be—how states of chemicals and electrical firings turn into your immensely complex subjective *self*. Fundamentally, you don't understand you, where you come from, or how you work. And yet, it is this same you that is trying to manage all of the complexities of being a *you* in the world and, for the most part, trying to be liked by all the other *yous* that it encounters.

Of course, it feels very nice to be liked. In certain cases, it is essential. Our wellbeing depends to some degree on the quality of our social relations, which requires us to be sufficiently liked by at least some people some amount of the time. The desire to be liked and the concern we have over what others think of us has a clear sociological and evolutionary purpose—to cooperate effectively, reproduce, cultivate a sense of belonging, and so on. The problem, however, is the tendency for this otherwise positive impulse to grow and mutate into a state of malignancy.

How often do we find ourselves worrying about what others will think of us before entering into a benign, low-stakes social interaction? How often are we worrying while we are in one? How often do we worry that others are thinking about some foolish but otherwise irrelevant thing we said or did in the past? How often are we doing or not doing things, buying or not buying things, trying or not trying things because of our concern over how others we barely know and are barely affected by will see us? Any and all of these common cases are where the concern over what others think of us can turn potentially malignant.

In infancy and early childhood, we are inadvertently conditioned by our parents, teachers, and other people we encounter to feel like we are the center of all attention, the most important thing in the world and beyond. Everything we do is relevant, consequential, or impressive. When we walk for the first time, it's the most important thing that could have happened in the world that day. If we draw on the wall, it's the worst thing. But of course, the world did not care about either of those things that day at all. As we age and are further socialized into the world, we slowly but surely realize that the world mostly has never and will never care about what just about anyone does, including us. We are not really at the center of anything at all, not even our own minds. We are not important in any grand sense. No one really cares. This becomes obvious when we turn our lens away from our self and toward how we view others. How often and how long do we think or care about others we don't know that well? How much do we care about the mistakes, missteps, and quirks of those we do? How often are we thinking closely about what others are saying or doing at any particular moment, or in life broadly? How often does it affect them if we are? Surely, there are some exceptions in certain circumstances with certain loved ones, friends, colleagues, and so forth. But for the most part, the answer is likely very little, if at all. We are all so worried about ourselves that we leave almost no time or mental space to worry about others in anything like the same way in which we are concerned. And so, likewise, most of the time, when we do or don't do something in a social moment or in life in general, and we are concerned that others will perceive us negatively, most people are in fact so busy concerning themselves with when they messed up or how they look to ever notice us, let alone care.

On the one hand, confronting how little others really care or think about us takes away some degree of our sense of importance; but on the other hand, it gives us the potential freedom to worry less about what others think and focus more on what we do.

In his famous twentieth-century play, *No Exit*, Jean-Paul Sartre wrote, "You remember all we were told about the torture-chambers, the fire and brimstone, the "burning marl." Old wives' tales! There's no need for red-hot pokers. Hell is other people!" This line, "Hell is other people," is perhaps one of Sartre's most famous quotes as well as one of his most misrepresented. He is not suggesting that other people are inherently evil or bad or unlikable, but rather, that hell is the imposed state of dependance and modification of one's self according to the integration, approval, and satisfaction of other people's perception.

For Sartre, we naturally identify our sense of self through what he referred to as *the look*, which essentially refers to the experience of knowingly being in other people's gaze or perception. In a sort of *self-reflective* function of consciousness, Sartre argued that a full comprehension of our self forms as a result of our perceiving that we are being perceived by others. He would refer to this construction of self as *the other*. At some level, in every encounter with another person, we become aware that others, like us, are constructing their own worlds and their own versions of us, rendering us into objects of their perception. As a consequence, since we are partly comprehending ourselves through the reflective function of this, we yearn for that reflection of us to be of high esteem and value, and we modify ourselves accordingly. Sartre suggested, however, that in the process of trying to fashion ourselves according to how we fit into *the look*, or minds of other people, we deviate from our free, personal, and subjective self. In doing so, we enter into a state of a sort of existential hell. In needing other people's approval of our self so badly, we relinquish our self in the process. Moreover, if one is not how they portray themselves to be or does not like something they claim to like, but acts as if they do, they are giving off a false impression to those to whom they display this behavior, all the while harboring an entirely different truth that will either die inside them or grow and fester into some eventual external explosion, unfairly putting those who were not given the right information right in the line of fire.

Ultimately, the truth is that no matter who you are and what you do, some people will not like you—just like how you won't like some people. Everyone is to some extent unlikable. We are all messes, hovering around inside these obscure brains, trying our best to try our best, tripping up on every third step. We are not the calm, cool, collected types of people we draw up in the ideal. "Even on the highest throne in the world, we are still sitting on our ass," wrote Montaigne. And so, if we're going to look weird or be unliked when we worry about what others think and attempt to mold ourselves accordingly, you might as well be weird and unliked just going about yourself as you are, as best you can.

Although it's easy to agree with this conclusion, that of course does not mean the actions that follow are easy to carry out. Arguably, to stop worrying about what others think of you, in this sense, is not the kind of thing that can easily be trained or rationalized away. When the anxiety of disappointment or rejection comes into play at the onset of various life choices, when the self-aware anxiety hits in the moments of certain social interactions, the uncontrollable state of mind that occurs seems to struggle to see order, self-control, and rationality. One can know all of the aforementioned to be true—that, in most cases, it generally doesn't matter what others think of you, that your life is lived and experienced through your own mind and your own mind alone—but just like an irrational fear of a harmless spider, irrational anxieties about harmless social relations and interactions, by definition, don't respond well to what you rationally know.

If there is to be some particular mindset that might help, though, it perhaps starts with subtle reminders—reminders of whatever helps regain perspective about how little others care, how little the world cares, how absurd it is to be and function as what you are, and that any moments of clarity, coolness, and success, when they come, are to be appreciated for what they are: unusual, heroic transcendental moments of victory over the norm of the human condition.

If, like Sartre suggests, we see ourselves by being seen by others, or as Charles Cooley put it, "I am not who you think I am; I am not who I think I am; I am who I think you think I am," then perhaps we must see how other people see as carefully and as generously as we can.

THE ART
OF TRUSTING
ONE'S SELF

The Philosophy of
Ralph Waldo Emerson

Writer, lecturer, and philosopher Ralph Waldo Emerson is regarded as one of the primary founders of American literature and can be credited with inspiring many subsequent prolific writers, writing styles, cultural perspectives, and philosophical movements.

Emerson was born in 1803 in Boston, Massachusetts, to Ruth Haskins and William Emerson, a Christian minister descending from a line of ministers. During his adolescence, Emerson studied at Harvard University, and following graduation, he would go on to teach at his brother's school for young women. After several years of teaching, he would then enroll at the Divinity School at Harvard to train to become a pastor. In 1829, he was ordained into Boston's Second Church and would spend the following three years or so as a pastor. During this time, however, Emerson would find an increasing sense of detachment from and disagreement with traditional religious orthodoxy. Specifically, he found that contemporary Christianity countered and sedated the very essence of human spirituality that it was supposed to inspire. Around three years after becoming a pastor, and about one year following his first wife's young death of tuberculosis, Emerson resigned from the church. "I have sometimes thought that, in order to be a good minister, it was necessary to leave the ministry," Emerson wrote in his journal.

Following his stint as a pastor, Emerson spent the next few years writing and publishing his first major essays while developing his career as a public lecturer. He would make his first significant mark on the public with controversial lectures, in which he suggested the value of separating from commonly held religious ideas and traditions, and in their place, argued for introducing new independent, forward thinking that relied on the *self* for divine experience and understanding.

During the following decades, Emerson continued giving lectures and producing several major, influential works of literature. He would soon become recognized as one of the mid-nineteenth century's leading writers and thinkers, inspiring individuals like Henry David Thoreau, Friedrich Nietzsche, Walt Whitman, Emily

Dickinson, as well as the philosophy of transcendental-ism, of which Emerson is regarded as the father.

Emerson's philosophy can perhaps be best explained in two of his most famous essays: *Nature*, published in 1836, and *Self-Reliance*, published in 1841. In these two works, Emerson primarily discusses man and nature being a unified, singular whole, the value of trusting one's own intuition and sense of reality, and the realization and forthright expressions of one's unique greatness and truth. More specifically, Emerson argued that all of nature is an expression and permeation of one metaphysical essence of the universe, or God, and that we are all both the expressions and expressors of this singular oneness. "Nature in its ministry to man," Emerson wrote, "is not only the material but is also the process and the result." In this, there is no sepa-ration between humanity and nature where humanity wills itself onto nature nor nature onto humanity, but rather, everything is essentially nature interacting with nature. Emerson wrote:

> Standing on the bare ground my head bathed by the blithe air and uplifted into infinite space, all mean ego-tism vanishes. I become a transparent eyeball; I am nothing; I see all; the currents of the Universal Being circulate through me; I am part or particle of God.

For Emerson, the distinction between the trees, the bugs, the dirt, and the stars is all but a phenomenal dis-tinction, not necessarily a real one. Rather, he believed that God is one thing found in everything and through everything—every object, every individual, and every particle of existence in the eternal now. As such, for Emerson, the transcendent spiritual experience is not found in any outward, previous, or future source, but within the individual in any given moment—moments where one's own mind illuminates the common features of the surroundings with potency, beauty, and interconnectedness.

Alongside this, Emerson also asserted that nature is in a constant state of flux, and that we must live in synchronization with its process, trusting our own intuition and flowing with the changing self. In order to do this, we must not hold ourselves to ideas, beliefs, or traditions of the past, including our own. Rather, Emerson suggested that our state is subject to change, and consequently, that we might feel or think one way today, but the opposite way tomorrow. Instead of fighting this, however, Emerson argued that we must lean into it. "No man," he wrote, "can antedate his experience or guess what faculty or feeling a new object shall unlock, any more than he can draw today the face of a person whom he shall see tomorrow for the first time." In other words, no one can know what life will be like tomorrow nor what such life may cause one to think or feel. However, one must move with it and live according to the present now. Out of this emerges what is perhaps Emerson's most popular concept, known as *self-reliance*.

Emerson argued that we often neglect to ever realize the unique perspective and greatness that comes from our particular culmination of experiences and states—not because we don't have access to such greatness, but because we are often held back and pulled away from it by others and systems of convention. For Emerson, great artists, thinkers, and writers aren't necessarily great merely because they have access to any higher, exclusive source of information or being, but because they are willing to address and express candidly what they feel in any given moment of life, despite how it might compare to the apparent norm. In doing so, they reveal not only their unique take on the world, but also the thoughts and sensations hidden within a great many others who feel the same. Arguably, great artists and writers aren't popular because they say something no one has thought of or experienced before, but because they say something that most of us have but weren't sure we were right in doing so. Emerson believed that for the sake of one's work and sense of self, the individual must rely on themselves alone and recognize that what they feel and think is real and legitimate. In a very Cartesian way of thinking, if we can know anything at all, it is merely that we exist. And if we can suppose anything at all, it is merely our own experience. This does not disparage our sympathy for others, others' ideas, or our connection with the natural world, but rather, it serves to prevent the disparagement of our self amidst it all. It serves to promote trust in our own interpretations and experiences, and it encourages us to express their individual merit.

In subtle contrast to Emerson, it is reasonable to also argue that perhaps there are variations in the resources and conditions for each individual, and thus, each person's ability to trust and express themselves is not always equal. If nature and human is a unified whole carried out through a process of self-fulfilling change, is it not also possible that one's own ability to defend and tap into oneself is part of a natural order and fluctuation beyond one's will? This simply serves to beg the question that if we are all transparent eyeballs—nothings seeing everything—how much say do we have in how much vision we have? Perhaps Emerson's concept of self-reliance can still exist in harmony with this question. Perhaps so long as one authentically stands in their own position of confusion and limitation, they have still remained in accordance with their own relative truth and greatness, and the notion of self-reliance holds steady.

Of course, like all philosophies and philosophers, Emerson's ideas in general aren't without flaws or counter arguments. "But it is the fault of our rhetoric that we cannot strongly state one fact without seeming to belie some other. I hold our actual knowledge very cheap," Emerson wrote. With this, Emerson himself suggested that he never spoke with any objective certainty or final truth regarding what he thought.

Self-reliance and individuality is not easy. It does not simply come from agreeing with poetic prose. To know and trust one's self in the face of consistent change, confusion, and a world that works to consolidate everyone is perhaps one of the hardest things anyone can do. And furthermore, although not always, certainly some of the time it comes with the risk of some amount of separation from others as well as conventional norms. However, perhaps the question one must ask here is: if all we can know and experience is our self, how can any life be lived fully if one denies themselves before even trying? If we hide or hinder ourselves out of the fear of rejection from others, are we not, in essence, rejecting our own self first; the only person we truly and inescapably have to live with? Emerson's work is a reinforcement and reminder of the importance of preventing this loss of self. It can help us attempt to live in the spirit of individuality, to raise the sail of one's own ship and use the unknowable force of the wind, always moving forward, finding beauty in the vastness that surrounds us, and creating our self anew.

UNCOVER YOUR TRUE SELF

The Psychology of Carl Jung

We feel as though we are in the driver's seat of our mind, driving according to our conscious will—but upon only a little introspection, we realize, at least in many cases, we are merely following a built-in navigation system that exceeds our knowledge and understanding. We perceive but the display screen of a complex system of software that runs on an even more complex hardware. If we do not attempt to familiarize ourselves with this navigation system, how it works, where it's trying to go, and how to override it when it sends us in the wrong direction, we risk aimlessly traveling the world, ending up somewhere uninteresting at best and disastrous at worst.

The twentieth-century Swiss psychiatrist Carl Jung is perhaps one the greatest and most capable minds that has ever attempted to explore itself from the inside and conceptualize a complete understanding of this sort of internal navigation system from the top down.

Jung was born in 1875 in Kesswil, Switzerland to a relatively impoverished rural pastor, Paul Jung, and a depressed, eccentric, spirit-seeing mother, Emilie Jung. Carl was a very introverted and isolated child who spent much of his time alone, engaging in activities of make believe, projection, dissociation, and analyzing the adults in his life. During early childhood, he strongly disliked and underperformed in school to the point of almost developing neurosis, regularly fainting to get out of it. However, as age and maturity would have it, as well as after his father expressed stern concern over his potential incompetence, Jung somewhat dramatically shifted to engaging more intensely in his education, reading actively on his own—in particular, philosophical and religious texts.

Following secondary school, after determining that he did not want to follow the family's path of a religious vocation, Jung would end up pursuing medicine at the University of Basel. After receiving his medical degree from the University of Zurich in 1902, he would work at a psychiatric hospital under the prominent and well-connected psychiatrist Eugen Bleuler. Several years later, he would leave the hospital and begin his own private practice.

As Jung became more successful and better-known in his field, he would get the chance to meet with the most groundbreaking and controversial of psychologists—a man who still holds this title today: Sigmund

Freud. The two met for the first time in 1907, on which occasion they talked for around thirteen hours straight. This would quickly develop into a strong friendship and professional association. They traveled the world and lectured together, analyzed each other's dreams, and discussed various aspects of their psychological studies and theories. However, Freud, being of a much greater professional stature at the time, as well as being substantially older than Jung, created a dynamic in the friendship that was much more like that of a father-son or teacher-pupil relationship. This would unfortunately pose problems as Jung's career advanced and began to encroach on Freud's. The two would soon find themselves in disagreements over fundamental aspects of each other's theories. Ultimately, these disagreements, Jung's tendency toward a somewhat mystical consideration of the human mind as opposed to Freud's more scientific, reductionist approach, the nature of their father-son relationship, and Jung's desire for professional independence, all caused the two to end their friendship in 1913.

Following this breakup, and as a consequence of it, from around 1913 to 1918, Jung experienced a sort of mid-life psychological breakdown. During this period, he spent much of his time introspecting and writing about psychological experiments that he conducted on himself, exploring the recesses of his unconscious. This period of transition, independence, and psychological turbulence would ultimately concretize his views of the mind and make his career as an independent theorist of psychology.

Put simply, the primary objective of Jung's work was to understand the nature of the psyche and then develop theories and methods to aid in the integration of all its components so as to create a singular, unified state of wholeness. In this context, the *psyche* simply refers to the complete personality of the individual, including feelings, thoughts, and behaviors—the combination of the unconscious and conscious minds. The continuous striving toward integrating the psyche through a process of self-realization and becoming a maximized, authentic individual, for Jung, was the fundamental goal of life and psychological understanding. ". . . man's task," he wrote, "is . . .to become conscious of the contents that press upward from the unconscious . . . As far as we can discern, the sole purpose of human existence is to kindle a light in the darkness of mere being." For Jung, there is a constant interplay between the unconscious and conscious realms of the psyche, which combine to create our complete personality. Most of this, however, develops and exists in the unconscious realm, beneath our immediate awareness and control. Thus, a significant portion of who we really are, what we really like and are capable of, and the reasons we do the things we do, persist within a realm we don't actively understand or have access to. And so, in order to come into a more authentic and complete state of being, the individual must attempt to make this portion of the psyche conscious by tapping into it and integrating it into the whole of their awareness. Jung would call this process *individuation*.

In order to better understand this, it is important to understand Jung's model of the psyche, which he divided, starting with the broader dimensions, into *consciousness*, *personal unconsciousness*, and *collective unconsciousness*. Breaking each of these three realms down, consciousness is the realm of personal awareness where one identifies explicitly and knowingly with themselves. At the core of this is another structure that Jung integrated into his model: the *ego*. The ego sits at the center of consciousness and provides a sense of personal distinction, creating the story one tells oneself about oneself in order to maintain continuity in their identity. The ego is expressed in the conscious realm by what Jung called the *persona*, which is the outward efforts of appearance that the individual actively displays to the world. This persona, however, is often disjointed from the individual's true self as it displays the character that one thinks or wants to be according to what the ego deems is appropriate to a particular society and role, not what is true to who the individual actually is. In order to execute and maintain this acceptable appearance and the sense of self-esteem that arises from it, the ego filters various components of personal experience and selfhood either into or away from the conscious dimension. What it filters away and restricts, it represses and sends down into the unconscious realm.

One of Jung's most unique and profound insights was to separate the unconscious into two distinct structures: the personal unconscious and the collective unconscious. The personal unconscious fits similarly into the ideas already understood and proposed by Freud and others of the time. In this structure, after the ego represses and disregards undesirable aspects of experience and selfhood, these aspects are stored and concealed in the personal unconscious, just beneath normal awareness. They still, however, actively affect and interact with consciousness. The collective unconscious, however, differs from the personal unconscious and other prior conceptions of the psyche in that, according to Jung, it contains and facilitates universal elements that are inherited through the sum total of human history—similar in some sense to how biological evolution works. Jung wrote:

> Man has developed consciousness slowly and laboriously, in a process that took untold ages to reach the civilized state . . . And this evolution is far from complete, for large areas of the human mind are still shrouded in darkness.

As a result of each generation of human offspring essentially imitating the behaviors of the previous generation (to at least some degree), an unbroken chain of psychological imitation has formed, going all the way back to the beginning of human history. Thus, a sort of reservoir of psychological predispositions, structures, and memories that has been formed by this chain is automatically inherited by each human being. Jung found this to be empirically demonstrable in both his own professional psychiatric practice, finding recurring similarities in the unconscious of a vast number of his patients, as well as in his historical and mythological research, which led him to notice that similar motifs, symbols, and themes that appeared in his patients' unconscious were also prevalent and consistent across art, myths, and literature within different cultures at different times in history, even if these cultures never encountered one another. In Jung's view, these shared motifs, symbols, and themes were expressions of the various psychic structures that are consistent across humanity, which he called *archetypes*. These archetypes, in Jung's model of the psyche, essentially form the basis of the individual's personality by predisposing them to specific cognitive tendencies.

Within the combined unconscious, Jung would refer to all the repressed, denied, and unknown content that the ego does not want to identify with as the *shadow*. Lastly, sort of nested within the shadow, is what Jung broke down into the animus and anima, which specifically refer to the suppressed feminine qualities in a male (anima) and the suppressed masculine qualities in a female (animus).

According to Jung, all the aforementioned structures of the psyche work together in active circulation to ultimately form what lies at the center: the *self*, or the combined, authentic totality of the unconscious and conscious. This self is who the individual actually is, what they actually desire, what they actually like, what they actually are capable of, and so on. Simply put, getting the ego and the persona as close to this as possible is the goal of individuation and, ultimately, a fulfilled life. Whether it's through methods like therapy, introspection, personal development toward authenticity, or some combination, ultimately, for Jung, it is the task of the individual to determine and strive toward this.

In all cases, this sort of self-realization requires an effort of radical self-acceptance; and radical self-acceptance requires an effort of radical self-honesty. In order to actively move deeper into the psyche, each time one examines a personal feeling, thought, or action, one must attempt to do so by accepting the complete and potentially undesirable truth of what it indicates about them—that they are not always who they think or hope they are. Each of these capital-ized-upon opportunities, personal or professional, is like a small step down the stairwell into the uncon-scious. As one goes further down, as they confront these deeper and darker elements of their being hid-den in the basement, they must, in Jungian terms, work to integrate their shadow—the full breadth of their potential faults and wickedness—as opposed to rush back up the stairs in denial. One's shadow does not disappear by looking away from it. In the same way that one cannot literally evade the shadow of their body by outrunning it, there is no move or evasive tactic that separates the individual from their psychological shadow. The danger, rather, is in the attempt to do so—the ignorance and denial of it. Jung wrote:

> Good does not become better by being exaggerated, but worse, and a small evil becomes a big one through being disregarded and repressed. The Shadow is very much a part of human nature, and it is only at night that no shadows exist.

Awareness of one's dark side allows one to more appropriately manage and recognize it when it sneaks up the stairs uninvited. One must know of a problem to be able to fix it, and it is an act of healing to admit that one is sick.

Although self-acceptance and authenticity is perhaps simple and obvious-enough sounding, the act of actually working toward radical self-acceptance and individuation is, of course, far from simple and obvious. In the absolute sense, it is almost certainly impossible. In the above average sense, it is still perhaps life's greatest and most difficult endeavor. To truly and honestly accept your weaknesses, potential evils, and shameful or unpopular interests and qualities, to admit that what you see, fear, or hate in others is or could be inside of you, to admit to yourself that you are not and will never be completely who you think you are and want to be, that you are not as virtuous as you had hoped, and to confront what your mind has worked a lifetime to keep from itself, is a task that shakes the very core of the psyche. However, it is perhaps proportionally essential for a fulfilled and complete life.

Ultimately, Jung's work provides insights, theories, and methods to help us move through this process toward not only potentially fixing the bugs in our navigation system, but also, in some sense, providing access to the controls, where now we can input the destination coordinates according to where we actually can and want to go.

THE ONE THING THAT CHANGES EVERYTHING

The Philosophy of Ernest Becker

Every sensation of hunger, every concern about our health, every passing siren of an ambulance, every tragic news story, every photograph of our younger self or the sight of someone aged into their last self, every leaf falling from a tree in fall—they all remind us in various ways that existence stands on a ground that can at any uncertain moment, and certainly at some, be cracked open, dropping us down into the abyss of non-existence. Forever.

Death is our lifelong opponent, always taunting us in the background, beating us up with each wrinkle, each gray hair, and each decaying function—if we are lucky and it is merciful enough to keep us around for a while. Like a tree, its roots sprawl down underneath existence, imperceptible to us on the surface, but yet, it is completely intertwined with it. Nearly everything we do is, in some sense, pressed up on by these roots: our actions, our beliefs, our values, our goals, our life.

In his book, *The Denial of Death*, twentieth-century cultural anthropologist and writer Ernest Becker argued that death, and more precisely, our denial of death, is the primary, underpinning motivational force responsible for the majority of human behavior.

As humans, one of the fundamental things that sets us apart from other earthly creatures is our unique ability to think conceptually. Becker argued, however, that although this in fact does set us apart and makes us feel as though we are special in some grand way, it does not actually make us so. He wrote:

> . . . man is a worm and food for worms. This is the paradox: he is out of nature and hopelessly in it; he is dual, up in the stars and yet housed in a heart-pumping, breath-gasping body that once belonged to a fish and still carries the gill-marks to prove it.

Consequently, humanity finds itself with this unique conflict: the juxtaposition of its awareness of itself and its condition, a living thing born to die like all other living things, and its lack of any reason to justify this awareness. Man is given no other significance for this burden he must bear. Becker wrote:

> What does it mean to be a self-conscious animal? The idea is ludicrous, if it is not monstrous. It means to know

that one is food for worms. This is the terror: to have emerged from nothing, to have a name, consciousness of self, deep inner feelings, an excruciating inner yearning for life and self-expression and with all this yet to die. It seems like a hoax.

Whether we are aware of it or not, according to Becker, this terror of death, and more specifically, our refusal to honestly respond to and accept it, is at the core of almost everything we do. And most of us are mostly unaware of it. The conscious mind cannot square the circle of the approaching abyss; it cannot make sense of the idea that this is its only serving of forever. In its inept confusion over its finitude into infinite nothingness, it fears it, it resists it, it uses the same conceptual capacity that allows it to comprehend its death to contrive methods and explanations to try to deny it. As Becker would refer to it, the individual undertakes a *causa sui project* or *heroism project* in an attempt to distract from and deny the implications of their mortality. We create and engage in symbolic constructs, cultural activities, and beliefs in an attempt to deny our cosmic insignificance and convince ourselves that we matter.

Becker suggested that people go about this in a number of ways, depending on the person. For some, it might be through religion. For others, it might be through different means of cultural contribution and status, like fame, fortune, a successful career, or the creation of things that are valued by culture. Every method attempts to eternalize the self either by a literal eternal afterlife or by the displacement of the self through an eternalized legacy and significance in the world that will endure beyond one's physical existence. However, Becker essentially argued that all efforts toward this causa sui or heroism or immortality project are futile and destined to fail. With the belief of religious afterlives and solutions increasingly being eclipsed by modern knowledge and understanding, man finds himself unable to do anything ultimately significant or immortalizing as the universe is revealed to be utterly chaotic, indifferent, and meaningless.

Becker offered no consolation in the way of resolving humanity's urge to heroism in conflict with its plight of insignificant finitude because he did not believe there was any. And so, what does one do from here? For Becker, it is not purely hopeless. What he offered, rather, was an alternative kind of heroism characterized by a sort of honesty about one's condition: living with an intense humility and positive resignation to the awe, mystery, and chaos of the universe and our insignificant position within it. This position—the absurdity of life and being made victim by our own death—can be framed in a way that does not deny it, but rather, provides perspective—honest perspective that can reduce one's concerns over the petty and trivial.

Potentially deviating or extending beyond Becker slightly, perhaps the best one can do in the face of death is to use it to put the life they have into perspective. Perhaps we don't think about it enough, at least consciously, to properly make use of it; to strengthen the muscle of our mind enough to handle its inevitable weight. When we consider somewhat often and hard that at some point none of this will matter and that it will all be lost, we shine a proportionally bright light on what does matter right now.

When it comes to life and death, there are really only two certainties: you will die, but you are alive now. Whether you agree fully with Becker or not, whether you believe in some afterlife or grand meaning, this is all anyone can truly know for sure. There is no telling if or what comes after death, there is no telling when it will come for you, but you can know that you are alive right now. To fully enjoy the present moment as often as you can and in as many ways as you can, to fall in love with a person, a thing, a moment, yourself, to make the most of everything despite knowing that you will lose it all to nothing, is more than enough heroism. What's worse than living a life knowing that one will die is living a life knowing that one will die without having lived as many moments as one can properly relishing in the fact that they have not yet died.

At some point, you will do everything for the last time. You will see your last sunset; you will taste your last bite of food; you will enjoy your last laugh; you will see everyone you know one last time; you will do anything for the last time; you will be you for the last time. If there is nothing specific to be done, the only thing that truly matters is that we do what matters to us while we can. There is nothing else to do, nowhere else to go. We must charge headlong into the absurdity, embrace the futility, and live hard for nothing in every moment.

One must be careful to not make the singularness of their shot at existence a pressure to get it all right—to do all the right things and think all the right thoughts and feel all the right feelings. The point is quite the opposite; you will mostly do a lot of the wrong things, think a lot of the wrong thoughts, and feel a lot of the wrong feelings. But precisely because this is your one shot at life, this must be ok. You are driving blind through the most impossibly complex, strange maze that you know ends in a head-on collision with a wall. What use is getting more upset or guilty about feeling upset or guilty in an existence that set you up? Of course, this is far easier said than done, but perhaps in true, deep contemplations of one's mortality, at least on occasion, this reminder can sometimes serve more as a sedative and not merely a stimulant.

WHY YOUR EXPERIENCE OF THIS IS ONE OF SCIENCE'S GREATEST MYSTERIES

There are trillions and trillions of cells that comprise who we are, all made up of the same building blocks of matter that make up everything else in the universe. And yet, there appears to be something very different in us, something unfathomably distinct from the countless other arrangements of matter. This seemingly singular thing is the only thing that lets us know that there are any other things, or an *in* or an *out* or an *us* at all. And without it, all things seem to disappear. This is, of course, consciousness.

Despite consciousness being so unavoidably essential to everything that we know and experience, and despite it feeling so intuitive and obvious, consciousness remains one of humanity's greatest unsolved mysteries. Unlike most, if not all other mysteries, consciousness is the only mystery that is in us—or perhaps more accurately, is us (at least what feels like us). It is the closest, most obvious thing to us all, and yet, one of the furthest things from our understanding.

Ever since the concept of consciousness entered the vernacular of consciousness itself, and surely prior that, individuals of all sorts have attempted to explain the strange feeling of being something that knows that it knows what being something feels like. Religious figures, scientists, philosophers, and everyone in between have taken their shot, but in spite of the fact that there have been substantial improvements in our knowledge of the brain, and various theories of mind have emerged, we still have yet to really get much closer to knowing what is truly behind the magic show of consciousness. If anything, the only thing that's been revealed is that we have mostly been looking in the wrong places, misdirected by the illusionist that is our own mind.

What we can say we know about consciousness is sort of what we all already know intuitively. Consciousness is this right now. It is what allows us to be aware of some portion of our external surroundings and internal states. And in our complex, human case, it is what gives us our likely illusory but no less strong sense of an inner eye—a director of rational reflection, focus, and comprehension. This might seem obvious, but that really just speaks to the point

of how little we actually know. Put slightly more elo-
quently, philosopher Thomas Nagel says that something is conscious if it can be said *that it is like something
to be that something.* As in, there is an experience had.

In slightly different, more specific terms, philosopher Daniel Dennett once said that consciousness is
like how the user interface on the screen of a smartphone works. In the same way the phone screen just
displays the results of a massive, complex layering of
electrical components working in the background,
consciousness is the display screen or user interface
of the brain, which results from the complex system
of neural subfunctions happening in the background.
Although this seems simple enough, there still remains
a deeply mysterious problem here. In the same way,
let's say, that the YouTube app cannot be pinpointed
in the electrical firings of the computer chips of a
smartphone, and essentially does not exist without
the screen, the experience of the events in consciousness cannot seem to be pinpointed in their relevant,
specific form anywhere else in the brain other than
in one's personal, conscious experience of them. In
other words, understanding the hardware, or brain
activity, serves only a slight purpose in understanding consciousness since only when the screen of consciousness is on and lit does anything in the hardware
equate to anything experiential. Thus, the perception of the screen has to be accounted for in order
to define or understand conscious phenomena, but
yet, this component seems exclusively subjective and

entirely hidden from anything outside the experiencer. As a result, there are many scientists and philosophers who believe that the nature of consciousness simply cannot and will not ever be understood (at least not in any complete sense). In this case, at best, it is like a puzzle that even if 'fully' put together, will only reveal an image that doesn't look like anything.

At the opposite end of the spectrum, religious types might suggest that the source of consciousness is already known; it is the soul. Or, along a similar train of thought, some argue for a theory of mind known as dualism, most commonly attributed to seventeenth-century philosopher René Descartes, which argues that the mind (or consciousness) and the brain are two distinctly separate things; that the brain doesn't create consciousness but acts as a sort of connection point between the physical body and some otherworldly, non-physical mental energy that interacts with it. However, for the most part, and for good reasons, dualism and other supernatural explanations of consciousness are mostly not taken seriously by many of today's leading thinkers. As a means of simply illustrating why this sort of non-physical, supernatural explanation doesn't work, consider the following question: can something with no physical attributes affect something that does have physical attributes? In simpler terms, can nothing make something move? Can a ghost both walk through walls and pick something physical up? Logically, it cannot do both.

As an example, in the case of the mind, let's say odorous molecules from freshly cut grass enter into a person's nose and, since these molecules have physical properties, they can bind with a specific set of olfactory receptors located in the upper part of the nasal cavity. This binding then generates and sends an electrical signal to the brain, which also has physical properties, causing the person to experience the smell of grass and inciting an associated state of mind—perhaps a nostalgia for spring. This then might cause them to physically react in a certain way, such as smile or inhale deeply. This, however, would require another physical signal to be sent from the mind to the parts of the brain and body that move the nose and mouth. But if consciousness is immaterial, with no physical attributes, how does it send this signal? How does the conscious experience of pleasure and nostalgia cause the physical brain and body to move and smile? The idea that consciousness is immaterial does not seem to agree with what we know to be true. As a result, it is now most commonly believed in science that consciousness is like all other phenomena, something that is to be considered from a naturalistic and physicalist view, made of matter with physical properties, part of the natural world, bound to the same laws of physics that govern everything else. The remaining problem here, though, and why it's not that simple, returns to the smartphone analogy. In the same way that knowing how the physical mechanics of a smartphone work would still leave someone with mostly nothing as a measure of understanding what a smartphone is actually like to use if they had never used one before, so too does the use of objective, physical terms to define consciousness leave out the essential subjective experience of it. To say, for example, that a physical interaction in the brain is happiness, neglects the fact that it isn't. Happiness is the feeling of happiness, not the objective, physical representation. And so, even if specific physical events could be pinpointed sufficiently as being the source of specific conscious experiences, it still wouldn't seem to make any sense as to how. How does the same, basic, non-sentient stuff that makes rocks and water and trees and worms, the same building blocks of everything else that isn't aware of itself, somehow come together in such a way inside you and suddenly, out of what seems like almost nothing, become your entire ornate awareness and experience of self and life? How does it become the feeling of happiness and wonder and romance and melancholy, the experience of colors and imagined intricate scenes that only exist inside your head? This overwhelming, perplexing sticking point is known as the *hard problem of consciousness*, a term coined by philosopher David Chalmers in 1995. In the words of Thomas Nagel, "If we acknowledge that a physical theory of mind must account for the subjective character of experience, we must admit that no presently available conception gives us a clue how this could be done. The problem is unique."

One other alternative theory worth mentioning is the idea that consciousness could be a fundamental property of all reality. This is argued for by the philosophy known as panpsychism, which essentially suggests that all things in the universe have a mind-like quality to them, and all physical systems, in a very loose sense, feel like something to be that system. It then follows in this theory that there must be a potential conscious quality in everything. Although counterintuitive and rather absurd sounding, this could still be a coherent theory within the bounds of scientific and rational understanding without throwing out any of the current frameworks of physics. However, even if this is true, it still doesn't necessarily answer the question of how to define or understand consciousness outside of the individually subjective experience, which again, returns to the same relative problem.

Ultimately, there really only seems to be two options: either the paste in our head creates this whole thing, or some ethereal transmission from some otherworldly dimension does. And both can only be described as unfathomably insane—a miracle in the truest sense. To be a thing that knows it's a thing, and furthermore, knows that it knows it's a thing; matter that knows what matter is; matter that can look out at all sorts of other arrangements of matter that have no idea what they are or aren't and give names and attribute feelings to these things; to feel pain and pleasure and love and happiness and all the rest; to experience, even if just for a time, this immense kaleidoscope of physical reality from the distinct and temporary home that is its head; if the rest of the universe's matter could look back at us, one can only assume it would cry with jealousy.

Like the concepts of infinity or nothingness, like the cosmic questions *why is there something instead of nothing* and *how did everything start out of nothing*, consciousness finds itself in the arena of humanity's most tightly sealed remaining mysteries. Only this particular mystery, this particular miracle of impossible dissonance, is you. And because of this, you are the only one who will ever know what it is actually like. Nothing will ever reveal your consciousness—your experience of blue, and love, and pain, and so on—to anyone else for all eternity. And it is the one thing that cannot be doubted. Nothing else can be known with certainty. But because you think, you are. And because you understand, you are some form of consciousness. It is the one thing you can always know to be true and forever exclusively your own. Your one, single experience of everything.

THE VALUE OF NOTHINGNESS

… when I think over the weirdest of all things I can think of, you know what it is? Nothing.

Alan Watts

Linguistically and conceptually, we know that nothing is the absence of a thing or things in a particular space. We might say that there is nothing in a glass when we mean that there is no liquid. We might say that there is nothing in a room when we mean that there are no items. And we might say that there is nothing in a vacuum of space when we mean that there is no matter or atoms at all. However, true, absolute nothing is perhaps something else entirely.

True nothingness might be nothing more than an abstract idea that doesn't really mean anything outside of language. Or perhaps, it might be a fundamental quality of all reality—a void with a function.

For obvious reasons, physics and quantum field theory look toward empty space as a definition and understanding of nothingness. One could study empty space by taking a fully sealed metal container and sucking out all of the air. Inside would then become a vacuum, void of all atoms and molecules. But when particle physicists do this and probe a vacuum, the space still actually contains quantum mechanical properties. These properties have the minimum possible energy a system can have and are in what is known as a zero-point energy state, which involves local quantum fields and virtual particles, but the point is, there is not nothing. There are things going on with measurable properties. Consequently, all the empty space of the universe isn't really nothing. As a result, science doesn't really take much interest in what true nothingness is and what its metaphysical implications might be because science doesn't really care about what it can't measure because how could it? But that doesn't necessarily make true nothingness any less relevant to everything.

In the words of theoretical physicist Sean Carrol, "It's probably better to think of nothing as the absence of even space and time, rather than space and time without anything in them." To try to consider this sort of true nothing, as in, to try to imagine the subtraction of everything in the entire universe, including time and space itself, one could theoretically do this and picture a sort of stark, black void, but of course, one would still be left with their self: the thing that is considering the absence of everything. Thus, by defining or imagining this, one is still ascribing a somethingness to nothingness—a thought and a concept is not nothing.

Naturally, because of the dissonance and strangeness of such an idea, nothingness can be rather intriguing, terrifying, or both. Also, of course, for some, the mere verbal construction *the concept of nothing* is enough to reduce the entire idea to absurdity. To try to understand nothing sounds obscenely unnecessary and foolish. And it might be. But what isn't then? To question why or how anything is is, at bottom, to eventually question everything. And to question why and how everything is is, at bottom, to eventually question nothingness. When followed to their end, all inquiries ultimately lead to these questions: why is there something rather than nothing? How? And is there nothing beyond it?

Many significant philosophers in history like Parmenides, Immanuel Kant, Hegel, Soren Kierkegaard, Martin Heidegger, Jean Paul Sartre, and many more; religious and spiritual ideas suggested in Buddhism, Taoism, and the very essence of the Christian God; research areas in science, especially that of physics and quantum field theory; all focus at least some of their discourse, effort, and intrigue on the mystifying potential relevance of *nothing*.

In some faint, strange, and sensorial way, throughout moments in our life, we have likely all come into contact with a sort of *metaphysical nothingness*. Philosophers like Kierkegaard, Heidegger, and Sartre suggested that we sense the nothingness through moods like anxiety, dread, or a dizzying nausea—a sort of premonition or awareness of the thin veneer of reality that hides the emptiness behind everything. We might feel this when we are alone at night and are having trouble falling asleep, or during a strange moment while having a meal or watching TV, or when we are somewhere out in public and something comes up that instills a certain anxiety in which we seem to suddenly realize that this all sort of just showed up out of nothing—and we will all be returning to that. And if that's the case, what is that nothing? Just on the other side of our skull and underneath everything we perceive as real, what really is that? What could possibly be the absence of all things, time, and space? We might contrive all sorts of ideas about an afterlife, but we have no reason to believe that it will be any different from what came before it. If our consciousness is infinite and there is an afterlife, then that same consciousness would have had to precede this life, which no one could possibly claim as a self-identifying person.

The philosophical view known as *idealism* posits that reality is, in some necessary way, linked with and dependent on cognitive perception and the understanding of ideas. This is not necessarily to say that the physical matter of one's body or things outside of one's body occur only in consciousness, but that one's knowledge of their reality only occurs in consciousness, and thus, their reality is dependent on consciousness. Even if one doesn't agree with idealism, one could still agree with the premise that our mind creates our sense and experience of being. And so, if our mind (consciousness) is lost upon death, then we are faced with a nonbeing of reality—a point at which we could no longer even imagine everything in the universe being removed because, as the imaginer, we would be too. This, of course, would potentially be absolute nothing.

It is strange and rather terrifying to consider that we can be something for now and nothing forever—but perhaps it is only because of the fact that we are nothing forever that we can be something for now. Perhaps only because of the negation of all other things across all other time and space, a being amidst everything else and nothing more, that we are something right now.

Following some semblance of the metaphysical train of thought of twentieth-century German philosopher Martin Heidegger, as well as Jean-Paul Sartre, the nothing comes first. Nothingness precedes consciousness, and the conscious act of negating, or imagining nothing, is an act that is derived from the nothingness. In other words, the nonbeing acts on being, allowing the intellect to negate everything except itself. For example, by self-identifying our self as our self, we have determined that we are our self minus everything else, which is to also say, we are who we are and nothing else. Our total sum of perceptions and understandings determined through the process of negating every individual thing from everything else consolidates into the final negation of self-knowledge. Nothing isn't the opposite of being nor what everything comes from, per se, but what allows something to be at all.

It is possible that nothing doesn't necessarily create everything but rather, serves as the backdrop that allows everything. Like a blank canvas is to a painting, nothingness is to the being of the canvas itself—and everything else. It could then follow that, at the risk of more seemingly rhetorical wordplay, everything and nothing are one, in simultaneous, interlocked coordination with one another; everything contained by nothing; nothing supposed by everything. As the blank canvas is to the painting, the empty glass is to the glass of water, and the empty room is to the bedroom, the nothingness is to all space and time. In the words of Alan Watts:

> So in this way, by seeing that nothingness is the fundamental reality, and you see it's your reality, then how can anything contaminate you? All the idea of you being scared and put out and worried and so on is just nothing. It's a dream. Because you're really nothing. But this is the most incredible nothing. So, cheer up! You see?

When we are tuned into this nothingness of being and truly confront it as a potential part of everything, it could and likely should be followed with a deep recognition of the thin temporariness coated over everything, and thus, the importance of focusing, not on some endgame, but on the very real implications that there are no endgames. The ever-fleeting present is all there is, filtered through us at the intersection of the mystical oneness of all things and nothing. And perhaps, as such, we should try our best to be careful of what we take seriously, and what we don't.

As long as we are, we cannot escape the everything

that is created through us nor the nothing that we created it from. This very creative intuition fills the poetry and art and literature and philosophies and religions and sciences and perhaps the general history of everything past and yet to come. We all share in this transient retreat to and from and through nothing. And thus, in the most rhetorically ironic yet beautiful way, we are all connected by nothing.

We might never know what nothing is until we know nothing at all. And even then, we might not. We are all free to imagine nothing however we like. Because if nothingness is in fact the source and destiny that connects us all, then perhaps, through nothing, anything is possible.

PART V

THE ART OF LETTING THINGS HAPPEN

I want to pause for a moment before we reach the final essays and briefly acknowledge the sheer difficulty of taking on the tasks that this book discusses— to find and create meaning in a life inherently void of it, to live well with oneself and others, and, more broadly, to live at all. These essays are not meant to suggest that these tasks or ideas are easy or simple to put into practice. The path I have traveled to find myself writing these words in this book was nothing close to a straight line. I have zigzagged all sorts of ways to find myself here. As we go about life, we are all inevitably going to encounter strange unforeseeable trapdoors, mazes, mirages, landmines, dead ends, and all the rest, no matter who we are and what we do. And so, perhaps as important as taking all this stuff seriously is not. It is a delicate, impossible balance—a tightrope walk with humility and meekness in one hand and conviction and pride in the other.

I feel it's important to acknowledge this and make it clear that the troubles and paradoxes of life line the crevasses of my brain, spew out my mouth, and wrap around my throat. I hope that my work often makes clear that it is not about escaping the paradoxical troubles of life, but rather, trying your best to live well enough with and through them, and then letting things take their course.

It is difficult to know how to do this, and it is difficult to maintain sanity while you do, but there are a few methods, ideas, and thinkers that I have found helpful in loosening up the tension and relieving some of the pressure. I hope the following essays help you, at least a little, do that as well.

THE BACKWARDS LAW

Why Happiness Is Ruining Your Life

If we are to be fully human and fully alive and aware, it seems that we must be willing to suffer for our pleasures. Without such willingness, there can be no growth in the intensity of consciousness ... to strive for pleasure to the exclusion of pain is, in effect, to strive for the loss of consciousness.

Alan Watts

The concept that Watts is discussing here is what he referred to as *the backwards law* (originating from Taoism), which argues that the more one tries to remove or escape the negative experience of life, the more negative it becomes. Rather, the more one faces it willingly and intentionally, the stronger and more equipped one becomes—the more meaningful and positive the pain and hardship can be made to feel.

Like gears, we are propelled by the revolving and ceaseless relationship between positive and negative experience. In fighting against their rotation, wanting happiness or pleasure all the time, willing to do any-thing to hold onto them or have more of them, in this, we only serve to jam up the gears.

Of course, there are exceptions to this. There are forms of pain and suffering and misery com-pletely overdrawn by our evolutionary ancestors and indebted to the unluckier among us in greater, worse, and malignant forms—forms of depression and anx-iety, fear and overwhelm, illness and poverty that are too far over the edge to be compensated by mere acceptance, mental stamina, or philosophical dis-course, without additional help. However, beyond this area of exceptional misery, there still exists a realm of suffering and unhappiness entrenched in human life that appears to be unshakeable, even when one's cir-cumstances are relatively good. This realm can draw the healthy, decent, prosperous person to self-hatred and self-sabotage, to addiction and suicide. It is the realm of misery in the background of any and every moment that should be enjoyed simply and happily but isn't. It is the mental pain that is specific to no one but applicable to everyone.

There is a struggle we each carry with us into all stages, all places, and all conditions of life. Inside us, there is a baseline of emotional and sensory experience that we ceaselessly return to, referred to in psychology as *hedonic adaption* or *the hedonic treadmill*. Because of this baseline, sometimes things will happen to us that make us feel extra happy. And sometimes things will hap-pen that will make us feel extra miserable. But as time passes, in both cases, regardless of any life event, most of us will return to feeling the same as we did before. Some of us have higher thresholds of happiness and positivity, but those some of us appear to be the least common among us. Even still, for those with higher thresholds, the discouraging nature of being cease-lessly destined to return to the same baseline state no matter what they do, remains enough to destroy the spirit if not properly padded with sufficient considera-tion and perceptual adjustment.

It is not hopeless. If we realize that the bad pro-vides the good, and the good provides the bad, we real-ize the contrast provides the life. Our baseline is not something to run from or dread or fight against, but it is something to appreciate for its constant renewal of life. In this consideration, we can perhaps reduce our self-inflicted, self-worsened misery by reducing our impossible expectation that the sole purpose of life is happiness rather than life itself. As a result, paradox-ically, it might be a little easier to be a little happier.

The hope for this, however, is not in the future. It is in this moment—the only moment—the moment in which there exists the chance to face and accept the gift of negativity and reduce the pressure on the soul's need to rid itself of it. The person who depends on their ability to accomplish away the struggle, sadness, and uncertainty of life, could accomplish the whole world just to be met with a disappointment so intense that it would destroy whatever is left of them. Perhaps, then, our quality of life is not found in the heights of our happiness or pleasures but in how we choose to consider and look at what surrounds these extremes, how we attempt to create a life of personal intention, meaning, and decency, and justify the inevitable lows rather than always trying to escape them.

Of course, none of this is to make light of how unfathomably challenging this is. There is temptation that looms in every corner, exploited by nearly every company, every cultural ideal, every aspect of oneself, all constantly alluding to the sense that this moment is never enough, and that there is a future where everything is perfect—if we just keep getting a little more of this or doing a little more of that. However, in the words of David Foster Wallace:

> If you worship money and things. If they are where you tap real meaning in life, then you will never have enough . . . Worship your own body, and beauty, and sexual allure, and you will always feel ugly . . . Worship power and you will end up feeling week and afraid . . . Worship your intellect. Being seen as smart. You will end up feeling stupid. A fraud. Always on the verge of being found out.

This same principle seems to also apply to happiness itself. If we worship happiness or pleasure, we will never feel good enough.

It's not as if by no longer worshiping happiness or things or articles of self, we will no longer feel things, want to do things, or want to accomplish things. Even if we wanted to stop trying or caring, we would not be able to do so easily. Just like how we don't have to worship the breath to breathe, or our hair to grow hair, we don't have to worship happiness or progress to progress and be happy. Like the inhale and exhale of each breath, the positive and negative flows in and out of us, constantly keeping us moving, progressing, and alive. Only when we hold our breath and try to keep all the oxygen in do we suffocate.

In every exhalation, there is a breath to come so long as we keep breathing. In every moment of hardship, pain, confusion, or weakness, there is a story taking place filled with the potential for triumph and vitality worthy of tears bursting with wonder and fondness for life, so long as we keep moving. So long as there is life in us, there is the rare and exclusively human opportunity to take this chaotic, thrashing existence, this strange nothingness, and make it something. There is the chance to connect and love and help, to feel and think and live, to experience the cosmic everything. And at some point, perhaps that is enough.

DON'T TRY

The Philosophy of Charles Bukowski

your life is your life.
know it while you have it.
you are marvelous
the gods wait to delight in you.

Charles Bukowski

Charles Bukowski was a twentieth-century American
writer and poet known for his unfiltered, potent,
and often crude takes on life. He was born in Germany
in 1920, and emigrated with his family to America
in 1923. Bukowski had a horrible childhood, beaten
regularly by his father starting at the age of six. As an
immigrant from Germany, Bukowski was ridiculed
by other kids for his accent and clothing, and treated
as an outcast throughout his school years. During his
teenage years, he developed a condition that covered
his face with extreme acne and acne-related blemishes,
further intensifying his self-consciousness and isolation.
The circumstances of abuse and loneliness imposed
on Bukowski as a young child and adolescent laid the
groundwork for his perspective on life and his desire

to eventually express himself as a writer. In an interview much later in his life, Bukowski said that his father was a great literary teacher because he taught him the meaning of pain, more specifically, "pain without reason." "When you get the shit kicked out of you long enough . . . you will have a tendency to say what you really mean," said Bukowski.

In his twenties, after two years at college, Bukowski would quit school and make his first real attempt at becoming a professional writer, bouncing around the United States doing short-term blue-collar jobs while writing hundreds of short stories. However, out of the hundreds of stories, only a couple during this time would go on to get published, and the ones that did found essentially no success. After a couple of years, he basically stopped writing all together, disappointed by the publishing process and his apparent inability to write well enough to be successful. He would continue to work various blue-collar jobs for several years thereafter.

In 1955, at age thirty-five, after about ten years of not writing, Bukowski nearly died from a serious bleeding ulcer. Soon after, Bukowski quit his job, which was at the post office, and began writing again.

A couple more years went by, and Bukowski would publish several pieces during this time. But still, nothing was providing much success, and he was forced to return to the post office job that he had originally quit. Unlike the first time around, though, Bukowski continued writing while at the post office. Before his shift, he would use whatever time he had to write. He would continue like this for many years, getting a collection of pieces published here and there in underground magazines, all with very little success. With no real sight of success or money or fame or even just making a living from writing, Bukowski continued writing nearly every day before work for years.

Of course, we know how Bukowski's story ended. He is being spoken about right now as a writer. A renowned, successful, and important enough one to be spoken about with significance decades after his passing—and to arguably be considered one of the greats of all time. However, Bukowski didn't end up becoming traditionally or publicly successful until he was into his fifties, many more years into the second stint of working at the post office. Only after a long, continued attempt at writing did his work finally become noticed and appreciated by an audience, and only after a deal with a publisher who agreed to fund his work did Bukowski begin to make any sort living from it. At fifty years old, on the tail end of the traditional career timeline, Bukowski got his first real shot and took it. After it would seem like it was over to many, it began. And not long after, he would become increasingly successful and famous in the literary world as well as in culture at large.

It took Bukowski years and years of writing and toiling and trying to finally have circumstances work out in his favor so he could find success as a writer—to get what he wanted since he was teenager and fulfill what he believed to be the purpose of his life. In this, it is at least initially perplexing that his gravestone reads, "Don't try." This message seems rather grim and counterintuitive, given his story. How could a man who became successful in fulfilling his idea of himself, a man who, although it took a while, found immense respect and recognition for his craft all because of his relentless trying, how could this man leave the words, "Don't try," as his final offering? Arguably, this is where the most important idea can be found, not only in Bukowski's work, but in his life.

In a letter to William Packard, a publisher, friend, and fellow writer, Bukowski wrote:

> Too many writers write for the wrong reasons. They want to get famous or they want to get rich or they want to get laid by the girls with the bluebells in their hair . . . When everything works best, it's not because you chose writing, but because writing chose you. It's when you're mad with it. When it's stuffed in your ears, nostrils, under your finger nails. It's when there's no hope but that.

In this letter, Bukowski is referring to what he believes separates successful writers, but he's arguably referring to concepts much larger: what allows for the development of purpose, success, and creativity in general.

When someone asked you for the first time what your favorite color was and you decided that it was blue or red or whatever else, perhaps it felt like a choice. But it wasn't really. No one chooses how colors make them feel and why some seem to paint onto the brain with better feelings than others. We can describe the reasons why we like the color we like, but we can't choose the reasons that affect us. The color sort of chooses us. In a relatively low-stakes situation like our favorite color, it's easy to just realize which one feels best and declare it without trying. How one defines their purpose and carries out the bulk of their life, however, is not so easy nor so low stakes, making it inevitably more complicated, convoluted, and challenging. Although, perhaps it is, at its core, somewhat the same as knowing your favorite color.

Bukowski constantly returned to writing throughout his life, never reducing or modifying his voice for the sake of something else. He never let the rejection or the suffering throughout the process ultimately take writing away from him. It's not that Bukowski didn't try, it's that he didn't try to be something that he wasn't. He tried to be a writer, but he didn't try to want to try to be a writer, nor did he try to write how he wanted to write. He just did it. And kept on doing it. In the same letter to Packard, Bukowski went on to say, "We work too hard. We try too hard. Don't try. Don't work. It's there. Looking right at us, aching to kick out of the closed womb." In this, Bukowski alludes to the idea that if you have to try to try, if you have try to care about something, or have to try to want something, perhaps you don't care about it. And perhaps you don't want it. Perhaps it isn't your favorite color.

At least creatively, we often perform at our best when we are ourselves, natural and honest, attending to who we really are and what we really want to say or do, without the addition of ulterior motives, without forcing it or overthinking. And perhaps this is, in part, what Bukowski meant.

None of this is to suggest that something as hard and complicated as purpose and passion and desire and success is easy or just a matter of being prescribed. Because it isn't. It's all as unclear and complicated as the very brain that contrives the whole system. And it's not as if writing, or filmmaking, or painting, or making music, or business, or whatever else must come easy to a writer or film maker or painter or musician or businessman in order for it to be the right thing or for them to be great at it. But it is likely, however, that if the pain and endurance of working through the process does not feel worth it, and you are not compelled to do it even in the face of rejection, hardship, or sacrifice, it is here where Bukowski might say *don't try*. But if it does, if the thought of not doing the thing hurts more than the thought of potentially suffering through the process of it, if the thought of a life without it or never having tried it at all terrifies you, if it comes to you, through you, out of you, almost as if you're not trying, perhaps Bukowski might say *try*, and "if you're going to try, go all the way."

WHY YOU (MIGHT) FEEL LIKE YOU'RE GOING CRAZY

"There are degrees of madness, and the madder you are the more obvious it will be to other people. Most of my life I have hidden my madness within myself but it is there," wrote Charles Bukowski. We all know this sort of madness—the sort that does not have a clear source nor a diagnosis. Not the extreme cases, but the more subtle kind that lurks within all the so-called normalcy of life. We traditionally only see and call it madness when it has finally reached its apex, breaking into the world in the form of abnormal behaviors that are past one's abilities, interest, or willingness to contain. But to at least some extent, some form of it is always there. We see it on the occasions when we don't quite recognize ourselves in the mirror. We feel it when we wake up from a strange sleep, and the room is coated with a dreamlike glaze of another reality. We live it when we look out at the world, up at the sky, down the street, into another's face, and experience a strange disquiet that we haven't the slightest clue as to what we are looking at. We know it when we try, when we fail, when we succeed, when a shoelace snaps or a tire goes flat.

There is that clichéd, overused saying, often attributed to Albert Einstein but was almost certainly never said by him, that goes, "The definition of insanity is doing the same thing over and over again and expecting different results." Regardless of its likely misattribution, it is fair to accept this as at least one accurate summation of a sort of insanity. But if this is true, is not life itself this? Is not everything in human life an endeavor with the goal of complete resolution, solace, reconciliation, control, peace, or happiness? All of which seem to be and have always been perpetually unsatisfiable and unobtainable. The human project is a continuous cycle of essentially trying the same things over and over and expecting different results. Madness is not the exception, it is the norm.

The loss of our early, youthful innocence marks the death of sanity. Not because we were saner as young children, but because there were no expectations for us to be. A young child spouting gibberish or running around with his or her imaginary friend is not mad, not crazy. They are a child. An adult doing the same thing, of course, is a madman. Thus, it is at this juncture of maturity where the expectations of sanity are enacted that madness is born. It is not behavior alone but the restricted nature of how we are expected to behave that synthesizes this sort of internal experience of a general madness. Only when the child in us is muzzled and clothed in a straitjacket do we suddenly feel this madness previously inexistent to us. We don't suddenly know perfect sanity, but we somewhat suddenly must act as though we do. What follows is a sort of sane insanity of life.

Every one of us experiences thoughts, desires, compulsions, or behaviors (realized or unrealized) that are, by all general standards, dipping into some depth of lunacy. "Men are so necessarily mad, that not to be mad would amount to another form of madness," wrote Blaise Pascal. Madness is perhaps one of the few words that accurately summarizes humankind so succinctly, simultaneously touching opposite ends of it—the good and the bad, the noble and the absurd.

The day-to-day requirements and expectations of social life—to be calm, certain, patient, responsible, impressive, rational, and all the rest—can, in any given moment, go against all the likely reasons to not be any of these things. We are made out of and live in the constant flurry of simultaneous electrical firings and chemical discharges of a brain trying to map a self onto a universe exploding with shifting matter. We sit at the end of this chaos, trying to narrow the ocean of time and space into a tiny, little canal. To successfully function at all, let alone impressively across a whole lifetime, is as much of a wonder as being itself.

This world does not budget well for its own insanity. It does not consider or pad itself well for mad people or the stable person's moments of madness.

The expectation of sanity arrives every morning at 9:00 AM. It awaits us in nearly every interaction. The fact that such a world, such a life, expects us to be sane is perhaps one of the most obvious examples of its own madness. We expect the world and the world expects us to be clear, to be lucid, to be rational, but that mad child is still inside all of us, existing with its relative stupidity, but denied the innocence to justify it. Perhaps, then, to some extent, we should be understanding and forgiving of ourselves as well as others if that child breaks out to blow off a little steam—if we act out of (or at least apparently out of) character, if we make jarring new decisions, if we lose a little grip, if we act a little foolish. There is a wisdom in this sort of general madness; a wisdom that reminds us that there are no right paths, no set directions, no certain answers, no dumb questions, that up is down and down is up, that the world is anything and nothing, that it's not that serious.

In the words of Carl Jung:

> Be silent and listen: have you recognized your madness and do you admit it? Have you noticed that all your foundations are completely mired in madness? . . . You wanted to accept everything. So accept madness too. Let the light of your madness shine, and it will suddenly dawn on you. Madness is not to be despised and not to be feared, but instead you should give it life . . . Be glad that you can recognize it, for you will thus avoid becoming its victim. Madness is a special form of the

spirit and clings to all teachings and philosophies, but even more to daily life, since life itself is full of craziness and at bottom utterly illogical. Man strives toward reason only so that he can make rules for himself. Life itself has no rules. That is its mystery and its unknown law. What you call knowledge is an attempt to impose something comprehensible on life.

WHY YOU WILL INEVITABLY CHANGE THE COURSE OF EVERYTHING

With a declining tendency toward religious faith and a diminishing sense of individual significance in systems of community, meaning, economy, and state, facilitated in large part by the increasing proximity to vast amounts of information, many of us unavoidably see ourselves as inconsequential specks destined to pass from dust to dust with nothing to show for it. In some sense, this may be true. However, there is one unique source of profound scientific-based significance that we all possess no matter who we are, what we think, and what we do. Without the requirement of any grand illusions of achievement or faith in anything beyond, everyone is born with this, woven into the very fabric of our relationship with reality; we wear it in every moment, and it cannot be taken off, not even by ourselves. It is the fact that each of us will change the course of everything forever.

Let's consider for a moment that time travel is possible, and you went back in time some significant number of years. If while you were there, you affected something, changed something, influenced something to go differently, stopped or started something that would have otherwise happened or not, even with just tiny, insignificant alterations, it would be highly likely that you would dramatically change the course of events throughout history. The proceeding future would potentially become a completely different one (or at the very least, a noticeably different one).

Most of us accept and understand this. It is the concern, fear, or premise of a vast majority of films, books, and shows that include time travel as a plot device. We recognize that affecting a small thing in the past can dramatically change the present, but yet, we rarely think about the way in which affecting a small thing in the present can dramatically change the future. Right now, without time travel as an option, reality still works the same way. In every present moment, your actions, interactions, influences, the stopping and starting of things, and so on, in some likely way, change the course of the future. Not every little thing we do always has a major impact on the course of events, but many likely do, and we do many things both big and small all the time.

This process of how tiny, insignificant changes can lead to huge consequences is explained by what is known as *the butterfly effect*, part of the branch of science and mathematics known as *chaos theory*. Chaos theory deals with systems known as *chaotic systems*, which react with high sensitivity to tiny changes in initial conditions. Through chaos, these changes compound and lead to the generation of completely different, unpredictable outcomes in later states of the systems. Chaos is sort of a misleading term because this process is not truly chaotic in a random sense. Chaotic systems function according to the laws of motion, physics, and deterministic principles like everything else, but because of their immeasurably complex factors and high sensitivity to minute variability in the initial conditions, they are just nearly impossible to predict, and they appear chaotic. Examples of chaotic systems include the weather, aspects of the brain, population dynamics, ocean turbulence, traffic flow, aspects of the economy, and so on. And of course, reality as a whole is a chaotic system; it is the total chaos of all the chaotic systems combined—the most chaotic system that a system can be. And of course, we are in this; a part and parcel of it.

As a simplified example, consider a scenario in which a person is living with a roommate. At around noon time, this person becomes hungry and decides to have a meal. From the options available at their apartment, this person decides to make a tomato salad, and they use the last communal tomatoes in the apartment. Later that night, their roommate plans to have someone whom they are dating over for dinner. They intend to make a pasta dish with homemade tomato sauce.

Before their date arrives, they realize they're now out of tomatoes and go to the grocery store to get more. When going to check out, by mere seconds, they manage to get in line just in front of another person. While checking out, the cashier mistakenly puts in the wrong code for the tomatoes and must clear and reinput the code, the transaction time now totaling about three minutes. While on the drive home, the person who was behind the roommate in line, now delayed by three minutes, passes by a car accident that had just occurred only a minute earlier. This person also happens to be an off-duty EMT, and after noticing one of the car accident victims on the ground, unconscious, they pull over, get out, and perform CPR on the victim, ultimately saving their life. This now-rescued car accident victim, just recently having gotten married, goes on to live a normal life and has two children. Eventually, one of those two children goes on to become highly successful in the medical field and creates the formulation for a lifesaving medication. As a result, thousands, if not millions of lives are saved, allowing more lives and families to continue and be born. Further events would then arise through these new individuals, affecting more events and more people, building and compounding over time into a massive web of sprawling cause and effect, interacting with other chains of cause and effect along the way, all still interlinked with that original tomato salad. Of course, all of the events in this story were also affected by many, many other moments where other things occurred according to other causes, but ultimately, based on the butterfly effect, the effects of that one roommate deciding to eat a tomato salad would, at least in some varying degree of causality, continue on until the end of humanity, perhaps the world, and perhaps beyond.

It is not uncommon to hear that someone wants to change the world. It is the tagline to so many people's dreams and aspirations. It's a noble and virtuous enough ambition. We should want to focus our efforts on intentionally doing as much good in the world as we can, trying to change it for the better. Perhaps, the more people who try, the greater the odds that we do. But ultimately, if one small action like eating the last tomato can potentially change the entire course of events in the future, what makes us think we could ever truly know the impact of our other actions? On the timescale of history, good, bad, and neutral events can never be fully known or identified. What we can know, though, is that our existence, although a seemingly insignificant fluke in a blip of time, through the butterfly effect, will fan out and leave a legacy with potentially increasingly dramatic effects for the rest of history. Chaos theory takes away the long-term predictability of our actions but gifts us back a perpetual role in reality's operation. Your legacy, albeit indirect and anonymous, will continue. It is a flame whose fuse is anything in existence.

This contemplation isn't a resolution of or replacement for a tangible, direct sense of purpose that arises through the day-to-day responsibilities of a job, career, passion, family, friendship, and so on. But it is to potentially serve as a supplement for those moments when some of the weight seems to suddenly drop out of these things and they feel illusory, futile, or temporary, and we question if anything we do ultimately matters beyond us, if we mean anything to anything else. In these moments, we can remember that we do—much more than we would probably even like.

In the final analysis, either no one matters at all, or everyone matters completely. There is really no in-between. No matter who you are, because of you, the course of reality's future will play out in a unique way. We are not only each the agents of our own story, but we are also the agents of the story of humanity, this earth, and perhaps beyond, collaborating on the unique expression of art that is the future.

CONCLUSION

In the end, I have somewhat ironically found my meaning in creating the contents of this book, as well as my other books, the Pursuit of Wonder YouTube channel, and *the pursuit of wonder* in general. The exploration and expression of ideas is one of the sources—if not the primary source—in which I find my meaning in life—where I attempt to embody the ideas I write about through the act of writing.

I hope and implore you do the same in whatever way you can and see fit. And I hope, even if just a little, my work has been of some value to you. If not, perhaps it functions like that of the sad song that reminds you, whenever you need it, *it's ok, we have no idea what's going on.*

Robert Pantano

BIBLIOGRAPHY

Aurelius, Marcus and Martin Hammond. *Meditations.* Penguin Books, 2006.

Becker, Ernest. *The Denial of Death.* Free Press, 1997.

Bukowski, Charles. *Love is a Dog From Hell.* Harper Collins Publisher, 1977.

Bukowski, Charles. *Betting on the Muse: Poems and Stories.* Black Sparrow Press, 1996.

Bukowski, Charles. *Factotum.* Ecco, 2002.

Bukowski, Charles. *The Pleasures of the Damned.* Ecco, 2008.

Calaprice, Alice, Freeman Dyson, & Albert Einstein. *The New Quotable Einstein.* Princeton University Press, 2005.

Camus, Albert and Justin O'Brien. *The Myth of Sisyphus.* New York: Vintage International, 1991.

Carroll, Sean M., Eleanor Knox, and Alastair Wilson. *"Why Is There Something, Rather Than Nothing?"* In *Routledge Companion to the Philosophy of Physics.* Routledge, 2021

Cioran, Emil M. *On the Heights of Despair.* University of Chicago Press, 1996.

Cioran, Emil M. and Richard Howard. *History and Utopia.* Arcade, 2015.

Cooley, Dennis. *Inscriptions: Prairie Poetry*. Turnstone Press, 1992.

Dullaghan, John. *Bukowski: Born into This* [film]. Magnolia, 2004.

Emerson, Ralph Waldo, A. W. Plumstead, and Harrison Hayford. *Journals and Miscellaneous Notebooks of Ralph Waldo Emerson, Volume VII: 1838–1842*. Harvard, 1969.

Emerson, Ralph Waldo. *Nature and Selected Essays*. Penguin Classics, 2003.

Emerson, Ralph Waldo. *Essays, First Series*. Diamond Publishers, 2016.

Gibran, Khalil. *The Prophet*. Alfred A. Knopf, 1923.

Jung, Carl G. *Psychology and Religion*. Yale University Press, 1960.

Jung, Carl G. *Man and His Symbols*. Dell Publishing Co., Inc., 1968.

Jung, Carl G., Aniela Jaffe, Clara Winston, and Richard Winston. *Memories, Dreams, Reflections: An Autobiography*. Vintage, 1995.

Jung, Carl G. *The Red Book: Liber Novus*. W. W. Norton & Company, 2009.

Kafka, Franz, Richard Winston, and Clara Winston. *Letters to Friends, Family and Editors*. Schocken Books, 1990.

Kafka, Franz, Anne Rice, and Joachim Neugroschel. *The Metamorphosis, In the Penal Colony, and Other Stories*. Scribner Paperback Fiction, Simon & Schuster, 1995.

Liiceanu, Gabriel and Sorin Ilieşiu. *Apocalypse According to Cioran* [film]. 1995.

Malone, Adrian. *Cosmos: A Personal Voyage* [film]. KCET, Carl Sagan Productions, British Broadcasting Corporation (BBC) (in association with) Polytel International, 1980.

Montaigne, Michel de and M. A. Screech. *Michel de Montaigne—The Complete Essays*. Penguin Classics, 1993.

Nagel, Thomas. "What is it like to be a bat?" In *The Philosophical Review LXXXIII*, 1974.

Nietzsche, Friedrich, Walter Kaufmann, and R. J. Hollingdale. *The Will to Power*. Vintage, 1968

Nietzsche, Friedrich and Walter Kaufmann. *The Portable Nietzsche (Portable Library)*. Penguin books, 1977.

Nietzsche, Friedrich and Walter Kaufmann. *On the Genealogy of Morals and Ecce Homo*. Vintage, 1989.

Nietzsche, Friedrich, Michael Tanner, and R. J. Hollingdale. *The Twilight of the Idols and the Anti-Christ: or How to Philosophize with a Hammer*. Penguin books, 1990.

Nietzsche, Friedrich Wilhelm, Thomas Common, Paul V. Cohn, and Maude Dominica Petre. *The Gay Science*. Mineola, NY: Dover Publications, Inc., 2020.

Nin, Anaïs. *Seduction of the Minotaur*. Swallow Press, 1961.

Pascal, Blaise and A. J. Krailsheimer. *Pensées, Revised ed. Edition*. Penguin Classics, 1995.

Plato and Harold North Fowler. *Plato in Twelve Volumes, Vol. 1*. Lamb. Cambridge, MA, Harvard University Press; London, William Heinemann Ltd. 1966.

Plato & Eric R. Dodds. *Gorgias*. Oxford: Clarendon Press, 1959.

Sartre, Jean-Paul and Philip Mairet. *Existentialism Is a Humanism*. Methuen & Co, 1948.

Sartre, Jean-Paul and Stuart Gilbert. *No Exit and Three Other Plays*. Vintage, 1989.

Schopenhauer, Arthur. *On the Suffering of the World*. Penguin Books, 2004.

Schopenhauer, Arthur and Konstantin Kolenda. *On The Freedom Of The Will*. Dover Publications, 2005.

Schopenhauer, Arthur. *Studies in Pessimism*. Cosimo Classics, 2007.

Seneca, Lucius Annaeus. *Epistles Volume 1, 65*. Harvard University Press, 1917.

Seneca, Lucius Annaeus and Richard Mott Gummere. *Moral letters to Lucilius*. Harvard University Press, 1925.

Seneca, Lucius Annaeus and Robin Campbell. *Letters from a Stoic*. Penguin Books, 1969.

Seneca, Lucius Annaeus. *On the Shortness of Life, 49*. Penguin Books, 2005.

The Buddha and Eknath Easwaran. *Dhammapada*. Nilgiri Press, 1986.

Thoreau, Henry David. *H. D. Thoreau: A Writer's Journal*. Courier Corporation, 1960.

Tzu, Lao, Dwight Goddard, Henri Borel, Aleister Crowley, Lionel Giles, Waler Gorn-old, Issabella Mears, and James Legge. *Tao Te Ching: Six Translations*. Start Publishing LLC, 2013.

Vonnegut, Kurt. *Breakfast of Champions: A Novel*. Dial Press Trade, 1999.

Wallace, David Foster. *This Is Water: Some Thoughts, Delivered on a Significant Occasion, about Living a Compassionate Life*. Little, Brown and Company, 2009.

Watts, Alan W. *The Wisdom of Insecurity: A Message for an Age of Anxiety.* Vintage, 1951.

Watts, Alan W. *The Essence of Alan Watts*. Celestial Arts, 1977.

ABOUT THE AUTHOR

Robert Pantano is the creator of the YouTube channel and production house known as Pursuit of Wonder, which covers similar topics of philosophy, science, and literature through short stories, guided experiences, video essays, and more.

youtube.com/pursuitofwonder
pursuitofwonder.com